Nurturing the Church

Nurturing
THE
CHURCH

R. PAUL CAUDILL

BROADMAN PRESS
Nashville, Tennessee

© Copyright 1989 • Broadman Press

All rights reserved

4213-98

ISBN: 0-8054-1398-7

Dewey Decimal Classification: 227.3

Subject Heading: BIBLE. N.T. 2 CORINTHIANS

Library of Congress Catalog Card Number: 88-39588

Printed in the United States of America

Library of Congress Cataloging-in-Publication Data

Bible. N.T. Corinthians, 2nd. English. Caudill. 1989.
    Nurturing the church : a study of Second Corinthians : a
translation and interpretation / R. Paul Caudill.
        p.   cm.
    ISBN 0-8054-1398-7 :
    1. Bible. N.T. Corinthians, 2nd—Commentaries.   I. Caudill, R.
Paul.   II. Title.
BS2675.3.B4913   1989
227'.3077—dc19   88-39588

All translations of Scripture are the author's, unless otherwise noted. Quotations marked (KJV) are from the King James Version of the Bible; those marked (RSV) are from the Revised Standard Version of the Bible, copyrighted 1946, 1952. © 1971, 1973 by the National Council of the Churches of Christ in the U.S.A., and used by permission.

Dedication

To the Christian churches that have effectively weathered the storms of internal strife and the influence of the pagan world by means of the grace of God and the dedicated leadership of the God-called apostles of Christ.

Analysis of the Epistle

I. Introduction and Thanksgiving (2 Cor. 1:1-11)
1. Christian Greetings (vv. 1-2)
   (1) Apostles
   (2) Saints
   (3) Church
   (4) Grace and Peace
2. Thanksgiving and Praise (vv. 3-11)
   (1) For God's Comforting Presence (vv. 3-7)
   (2) For God's Deliverance (vv. 8-10)
   (3) For Prayer Help (v. 11)

II. Paul and His Current Travel Plans (2 Cor. 1:12 to 2:4)
1. His Obvious Sincerity (1:12-14)
2. His Change of Plans (vv. 15-19)
3. The Promises of God (v. 20)
4. The Seal of the Holy Spirit (vv. 21-22)
5. Co-Workers (vv. 23-24)
6. A Personal Decision (2:1-2)
7. Paul's Love for the Corinthians (vv. 3-4)
8. His Forgiving Spirit (2:5-11)
9. His Journey to Macedonia (2:12-13)

III. The Ministry of the New Covenant (2 Cor. 2:14 to 7:1)
1. The Triumphant Leadership of God in Christ (2:14-17)
2. The New Covenant Relationship (3:1-18)
   (1) An Epistle of Christ (vv. 1-3)
   (2) The Ministers of the New Covenant (vv. 4-6)
   (3) The Ministry of Death and Life in Contrast (vv. 7-8)
   (4) Glory in the Ministry (vv. 9-10)
   (5) Hardened Hearts and the Veil (vv. 12-16)
   (6) Freedom (vv. 17-18)
3. The Treasure and the Earthen Vessels (2 Cor. 4:1-15)
   (1) Jesus Christ the True Life (vv. 1-6)
   (2) The Treasure and the Earthen Vessels (vv. 7-12)
4. The Role of Faith (2 Cor. 4:13 to 5:10)
   (1) The Seen and the Unseen (4:16-18)
   (2) The Earthly House (5:1-5)
   (3) The Pledge of the Spirit (vv. 6-10)
   (4) The Central Fact (v. 10)
5. The Ministry of Reconciliation (5:11 to 6:11)
   (1) The Fear of the Lord (vv. 11-13)
   (2) The Love of Christ (vv. 14-16)
   (3) The New Creation (vv. 17-21)
   (4) God's Fellow Workers (6:1)
   (5) Day of Salvation (v. 2)

      (6) Safeguarding the Ministry of Reconciliation (vv. 3-10)
      (7) Freedom of Proclamation (vv. 11-13)
   6. The Call to the Separate Life (6:14 to 7:1)
      (1) Mismated Marriages (vv. 14-15)
      (2) The Temple of God (6:16 to 7:1)
IV. Paul's Joy at the Response of the Corinthian Church (2 Cor. 7:2-16)
   1. A Plea for Acceptance and Understanding (vv. 2-5)
   2. The Coming of Titus (vv. 6-8)
   3. Godly and Worldly Sorrow (vv. 9-12)
   4. Love and Joy (vv. 13-16)
V. The Grace of Giving (2 Cor. 8:1-24)
   1. The Example of the Macedonian Churches (vv. 1-7)
   2. The Supreme Test in Giving (vv. 7-8)
   3. The Example of Jesus (v. 9)
   4. Readiness to Complete the Giving (vv. 10-12)
   5. The Principle of Equality (vv. 13-15)
   6. The Zeal of Titus and the Brother (vv. 16-19).
   7. Christian Ethics in Giving (vv. 20-21)
   8. Titus and Companion (vv. 22-24)
VI. The Offering for the Poor Saints at Jerusalem (2 Cor. 9:1-15)
   1. The Readiness of the Corinthians (vv. 1-5)
   2. Sowing and Reaping (vv. 6-11)
   3. The Ministry of Giving (vv. 12-14)
   4. Paul's Joy (v. 15)
VII. Paul's Defense of His Ministry (2 Cor. 10:1-18)
   1. A Personal Appeal (vv. 1-2)
   2. The Spiritual Warfare (vv. 3-10)
   3. Invidious Comparisons (vv. 11-18)
VIII. Paul's Defense of His Ministry Continues (2 Cor. 11:1-33)
   1. A Slight Tinge of Apology (v. 1)
   2. Paul's Deep Concern for the Corinthians (vv. 2-4)
   3. Paul and the False Apostles (vv. 5-15)
   4. The Matter of Boasting (vv. 16-23)
   5. Paul's Sufferings as a Minister of Christ (vv. 24-33)
IX. Paul's Visions and Revelations (2 Cor. 12:1-21)
   1. Visions and Revelations (vv. 1-6)
   2. A Thorn in the Flesh (vv. 7-10)
   3. Paul's Continuing Concern for the Corinthian Church (vv. 11-21)
X. Final Words of Warning and Greetings (2 Cor. 13:1-14)
   1. Paul's Third Visit to Corinth (vv. 1-3)
   2. Christ's Crucifixion (v. 4)
   3. A Challenge to Self-Examination (vv. 5-10)
   4. Final Exhortation, Greetings, and Benediction (vv. 11-14)

R. PAUL CAUDILL

Foreword

In this study, I have endeavored to help Bible lovers gain a better understanding of 2 Corinthians and to assist serious Bible students to gain a more comprehensive grasp of the full sweep of the divine thought and holy purpose of this incisive epistle.

In translating the Greek text I have endeavored to render the meaning of the words of the text in contemporary English with as much literal integrity as possible and without bias. I have not dealt with textual problems but have left such matters to others. The purpose of this work does not merit such an approach. For those desiring to pursue a critical study of textual nature, there are many responsible words that may be helpful.

In this translation I have endeavored to employ the grammatical, historical, etymological, sociological, and psychological approach, while depending upon the illuminating guidance of the Holy Spirit, apart from whom the greater implications of God's Holy Word cannot be understood.

The riches of God's Word are so abundant in meaning concerning the eternal hope and the contemporary life-style of the Christian that no amount of study can exhaust all the treasures contained therein.

The Analysis (pp. vi and vii) of 2 Corinthians is followed in marking the Scripture passages under discussion. The chapter headings do not always match the major Scripture sections of the Analysis. If this causes you a problem, please refer to the Analysis.

R. Paul Caudill

Contents

1 Introduction and Thanksgiving 15
   2 Corinthians 1:1-11

2 Paul and His Current Travel Plans 26
   2 Corinthians 1:12 to 2:4

3 The New Covenant Relationship 46
   2 Corinthians 3:1-18

4 The Treasure and the Earthen Vessels 55
   2 Corinthians 4:1-15

5 The Role of Faith 64
   2 Corinthians 4:13 to 5:10

6 The Ministry of Reconciliation 75
   2 Corinthians 5:11 to 6:11

7 Paul's Joy at the Response of the Corinthian Church 85
   2 Corinthians 7:2-16

8 The Grace of Giving 96
   2 Corinthians 8:1-24

9 The Offering for the Poor Saints at Jerusalem 108
   2 Corinthians 9:1-15

10 Paul's Defense of His Ministry 118
   2 Corinthians 10:1-8

11 Paul's Defense of His Ministry 128
   2 Corinthians 11:1-33

12 Paul's Visions and Revelations 139
   2 Corinthians 12:1-21

13 Final Words of Warning and Greeting 150
   2 Corinthians 13:1-14

Bibliography 159

Introduction

The First Epistle of the apostle Paul to the Christians of Corinth was in response to questions asked by the Corinthian Christians. It also dealt with the problems of low moral standards (ch. 6) and other troublesome matters that were disturbing the body of believers there. The Second Epistle of the apostle to the Corinthians was a follow-up letter in his effort to heal old wounds and to deal with other matters relating to the welfare of the Corinthian church. The first part of the letter amounted to a plea for reconciliation among the dissident church members, who were obviously in the minority. God in Christ was presented as the great reconciler, but the letter itself presents an inspiring example of true reconciliation among believers where the unity of the bond of love has been fragmented by serious problems within the church. And Paul himself became a stirring example of the loving initiative that a Christian leader may take in an effort to heal and restore the broken bonds of fellowship.

In chapters 10—13 Paul responded to the crass efforts of those who sought to discredit his ministry to the saints of Corinth. Paul stoutly refuted the disposition on the part of Corinthian dissidents to discredit his ministry and to assign him, in rank, a place below the so-called "super apostles." His effort to authenticate his genuine apostolic ministry left little doubt for question on the part of any who would discredit his mission under God.

The City of Corinth

Situated on the isthmus that connected the Peloponnesus with Greece, and lying between the Ionian and Aegean Seas, the city had long been famous for its commerce. In Paul's day Corinth was the capital of Achaia and the headquarters of the Roman proconsul (Acts 18:12). The plurality of religious viewpoints, as well as the large number of adherents in Corinth, exposed the Corinthian believers to many corrupting influences. The worship of Venus and the alleged employment of female slaves in the service of strangers gave the city a bad name and caused the

11

expression "to Corinthianize" to become proverbial in reference to the wanton life-style.

Occasion and Purpose

The antagonism of Paul's mission to the Gentiles, and his authority as a called apostle, had reached a crucial point. Even though the critics were a minority group, it was necessary for Paul to respond to the opposition openly. He had to vindicate his role as an apostle of Jesus Christ.

At the heart of the moral problems was an incestuous relationship (1 Cor. 5:1ff.), but Paul failed to mention the name of the offender. It seems that the church members had condoned the nauseous incest to the point that Paul felt it necessary to call for the church to discipline him. Apparently the church heeded his words and disciplined the offender; then Paul manifested the true spirit of forgiveness in his further instruction concerning the offender. The time of the offense is really not important to the issue though it is likely that it occurred after the writing of the First Epistle, since there was no mention of the particular offense in that letter.

Paul's first visit to Corinth took place at the founding of the church. Then apparently followed the "painful visit" (2 Cor. 2:1). He was ready now to make the third visit (13:1) at which time he would be unsparing in his rebuke of any others whose life-style might defame the church.

Paul did not deal with the precise nature of the criticism directed against him, which was at least insulting. One may gain, however, some idea about the criticism by referring to certain passages in the Epistle: 1:15ff.; 3:1ff.; 4:3; 10:1ff., 7, 13ff.; 11:7ff.; 12:12; and 13:3.

Part of the opposition seemed to come from Jewish Christians from Palestine who tried to leave the impression that they were "super" apostles (12:11). There is nothing to indicate that these so-called "apostles" had been sent by the Jerusalem church to stir up opposition against Paul. Whatever their approach, in their opposition to Paul, and whatever their relationship to the influences of gnosticism, they were rabid enemies of Paul and were a part of the occasion and purpose of the Epistle.

There has been much discussion of exegetes concerning the authenticity and unity of 2 Corinthians, but in all the dialogues there has been no disposition, so far as I know, to set aside the Pauline authorship of the Epistle. And the question as to whether chapters 10—13 might have preceded chapters 1—9 is hardly significant to the overall thrust of the Epistle.

The authenticity of the Pauline authorship of the Second Epistle to the Corinthians is widely acclaimed, and few would contest it. Many expositors have dealt with the problem of the unity of the Epistle in detail, but the argument against the unity of the Epistle seems to be illogical and superficial. I prefer to uphold the unity of the Epistle as do a host of scholars who have gone before. So far as my effort is concerned here, I prefer to leave such questions to others and to deal with the central topics of the Epistle and the relevancy of those topics to the contemporary Christian and his church.

Time and Place

Many exegetes date 1 Corinthians in the spring of AD 55 (see 1 Cor. 16:8). Certainly Paul was in Macedonia at the time he wrote the letter (2:12). Some identify the letter with the occasion of the uproar in Ephesus incited by the silversmiths as related in Acts 19—20. After the uproar, Paul went to Macedonia and from there to Greece. Since the distance between Ephesus and Corinth was not great, Paul's experiences there might well have taken place during a very short time, maybe six to eight months, rather than eighteen months as some scholars hold. In this case, the letter might be dated in the autumn of AD 55.

The Overall Thrust of the Epistle

How shall one attempt to define the thrust of an epistle such as 2 Corinthians? There are so many facets to the varied topics of fruitful meaning in the Epistle to the Corinthians and thereby to the churches of all succeeding generations. Even a cursory glance at Paul's words give rise to a plethora of themes, any one of which might be related to the thrust of the Epistle. The following are among the many thoughts that arise: victory in Christ, guidelines for churches, the glory of the ministry, guidelines for the pastor and people, discipline in the church, triumph over trouble in a church, Christ and the troubled church, etc.

Over all of the multifacets of topics of Paul's message to the Corinthian church there seems to appear the overall theme of nurturing the church. Nurturing the church in times of trouble; nurturing the church in the stewardship of substance in relation to the poor saints; nurturing the church in the understanding of the ministry of the New Covenant; nurturing the church in its regard for the authentic character of the called ministers of the gospel of Christ; nurturing the church in her comprehension of the role of faith on the part of believers and the relationship of faith to works!

Paul's Second Epistle to the Corinthians contains the elements of a handbook for pastors and people, a handbook graciously intertwined with the divine teaching that relates to the varied aspects of the Christian's pilgrimage on earth—the pilgrimage of believers of every generation of all the ages.

2 CORINTHIANS 1

¹Paul, an Apostle of Jesus Christ through the will of God, and brother Timothy, to the church of God that is at Corinth, together with all the saints who are in the entire region of Achaia,

²grace to you and peace from God our Father and our Lord Jesus Christ.

³Blessed be the God and Father of our Lord Jesus Christ, the Father of Mercies, and God of all encouragement,

⁴who cheers us up in our every tribulation so that we may be able to cheer up others in every tribulation with the encouragement with which we ourselves are encouraged by God.

⁵For just as the sufferings of Christ overflow unto us, even so, through Jesus Christ, our consolation overflows.

⁶But whether we are afflicted, it is in behalf of your encouragement and salvation; or whether we are comforted, it is in the interest of your encouragement which manifests itself in the patient endurance of the same sufferings which we ourselves are experiencing.

⁷And our hope concerning you is unchangeable, knowing that as you are sharers of our sufferings, so also are you of the consolation.

⁸Certainly we do not want you to be ignorant, brothers, concerning our affliction that took place in Asia, that we were burdened altogether beyond our strength, so that we despaired even of life,

⁹but we ourselves have had within ourselves the sentence of death, that we should not trust in ourselves but in God, who raises the dead;

¹⁰who delivered us from so great a death, and will continue to deliver us; in whom we have set our hope that He will keep on delivering us in the future.

¹¹Also, you help by joining in prayer for us, so that the favor which you do may be bestowed upon us through the prayers of many people.

¹²For our boasting is this: the testimony of our consciousness, that it is in the holiness and purity of God, not in fleshly wisdom but in the grace of God, we conducted ourselves in the world, and all the more toward you.

¹³For we are not writing anything to you other than what you read and understand, and I hope you will continue to understand to the end.

¹⁴And just as you did partially understand us that, even as we are your glorying, you are also ours in the day of our Lord Jesus.

¹⁵And with this confidence, I decided to come to you earlier, that you might have a second favor,

¹⁶and to pass through you to Macedonia, and again from Macedonia to come to you, and by you to be helped on my journey to Judea.

¹⁷In making this decision, therefore, did I consequently act in fickleness? Or the plans I make, do I make them according to the flesh, that there should be with me the Yes, Yes and the No, No?

¹⁸But since God is faithful, our word to you is not an ambiguous Yes and No.

¹⁹For God's Son, Christ Jesus, who was proclaimed among you through us, through me and Silvanus and Timothy, was not an ambiguous Yes and No, but rather in Him was the Yes.

15

[20]For, as many as are the promises of God, in Him is the Yes; therefore, through Him also is the Amen to God, unto His glory through us.

[21]Now he that keeps on strengthening us together with you in Christ, and has anointed us, is God,

[22]who also has marked us with His seal and given us the first installment of the Spirit in our hearts.

[23]And I call upon God as a witness against my soul that, intentionally sparing you, I came not again to Corinth.

[24]It is not that we are lording it over your faith, but that we are co-workers for your joy; for it is by your faith that you stand.

1

Introduction and Thanksgiving

2 Corinthians 1:1-11

Paul's plans concerning the postponement of his intended visit to Corinth leave the reader of 2 Corinthians with some difficulty because of the absence of more specific information concerning the proposed visit and his cancellation of his plans. Evidently the Corinthian reader would not need further explanation of all the facts involved, even though some of them failed to understand Paul and his change of plans. Apparently Paul had planned to make two visits to Corinth but canceled the first visit for reasons he explained later. His first plan seemed to call for a visit to Corinth on his way to Macedonia and for another visit on his way back from Macedonia in the hope that he would gain support from the Corinthians to help him on his way to Judea. Paul, for reasons all his own, wanted to change his plans and apparently some of the Corinthians used this as a basis for attacking the integrity of his purpose. But whatever the basis of the furor to his change of travel plans, Paul stoutly defended the sincerity of his purpose and his integrity.

Is it not possible that Paul's change of plans may have been occasioned by problems at both Ephesus and Corinth and by a desire on his part for a longer "cooling off" period following his severe words of rebuke in his first Corinthian letter? Following brief words of greeting (1:1-2) Paul offered words of thanksgiving for God's consolation and sympathy, defended his sincerity of purpose, and explained the reason for the postponement of his visit.

1. Christian Greetings (vv. 1-2)

> Paul, an Apostle of Jesus Christ through the will of God, and brother Timothy, to the church of God that is at Corinth, together with all the saints who are in the entire region of Achaia, grace to you and peace from God our Father and our Lord Jesus Christ.

(1) Apostles

Although Paul is not mentioned by Mark and is not referred to in the Acts as an apostle, Paul regarded himself as an apostle of Jesus Christ no less than the others who were so named in the Gospels. For that matter, in the choice and the naming of the original twelve, there is nothing in the Scriptures to suggest that there would be no other apostles. Note that Paul did not refer to Timothy as an apostle, but rather as a "brother" in Christ. Timothy, Paul's "son" in the ministry, came from a Christian home in Lystra (Acts 16:1). His mother was a Christian and likewise his grandmother (2 Tim. 1:5). The close ties that existed between Paul and Timothy made for a happy relationship in their mutual efforts in the furtherance of the gospel.

(2) Saints

The word "saints," which Paul used here, means *holy, set apart unto God and for God*. The meaning of the word further issues in the meaning of *purity, uprightness, separateness*. All believers who have been born again are to be regarded as saints. They are people who have made a personal confession of faith in Jesus Christ based on repentance and the revelation of Christ's redeeming love as experienced in their own lives and who have set apart their lives unto God and for God's use in all their ways. The age of the believer has nothing to do with the term "saint." All of the saints of Corinth and the whole of Achaia were included in the address of the Epistle, and the admonitions of God's Word to believers are to be heeded by all believers. The disturbing life-styles of many Christians in contemporary society are due to the fact that many of them are "selective" in their individual responses to God's commands. And this is why there is such diversity in the life-styles of believers.

(3) Church

The word "church" occurs nine times in 2 Corinthians. The plural form occurs in eight other passages. Paul used the word "church" *(ekklēsia)* to relate to a local church or local community of believers. In 11:28 his expression "all the churches" was a clear reference to the close relationship of the respective bodies of believers to each other. The expression "the church of God" appears also in 1 Corinthians 1:2 and includes every assembly or "house group" or body of Christians. Paul's reference to Achaia indicates that his message was intended to be a circular letter and to reach all other believers in the political area which in AD 27 embraced the whole of Greece. The scattered Christian must have been widely dispersed in the area for the churches named were in Corinth, Athens, and Cenchrae (Rom. 16:1).

(4) Grace and Peace

Note in verse 2 the order of the words "grace and peace." The words are found invariably in this order in the epistles of Paul. Grace *(charis)* is a "lovely, unmerited, God-given experience of His favoring presence felt in the life of man." One can have peace only after he has received "grace" (Caudill, *Ephesians*). The word "peace" *(eirēnē)* calls to mind the word *shalom* used by ancient Hebrew scholars. "The word means 'well being under God's sovereign rule.' That tranquil state of mind and heart that is independent of circumstance and that results from being in Christ and in doing God's will in all things" (ibid.).

2. Thanksgiving and Praise (vv. 3-11)

(1) For God's Comforting Presence (vv. 3-7)

Blessed be the God and Father of our Lord Jesus Christ, the Father of Mercies, and God of all encouragement, who cheers us up in our every tribulation so that we may be able to cheer up others in every tribulation with the encouragement with which we ourselves are encouraged by God (vv. 3-4).

The words "blessed be God" are the words used by Jews whenever they speak of God. Paul's repeated use of the word "tribulation" and of the word "sufferings" refers to the trials which he had at the hands of his enemies, trials which appeared to be still going on. These trials were grave and carried the threat of death, which did eventually come to him. Paul dwelt upon his own sufferings and those of other believers because their sufferings related directly to the sufferings of Christ who, in the flesh, suffered even unto death as Paul was one day to suffer. Paul had a burning desire to know Christ more fully, to achieve His lifestyle, and also to share in His sufferings.

Was the apostle Paul really terrified by his sufferings? He certainly did not reach despair. Just as Jesus at times avoided the vicious effort on the part of His enemies to put Him to death prematurely—that is, before He had accomplished His mission on earth—so it was with the apostle Paul. God had committed to him a mission among the Gentiles (Acts 9:15-16), and Paul did not want it to end prematurely.

Paul's *tribulations* (vv. 3-4) were simply the acts of harassment and physical violence which he constantly experienced at the hands of his adversaries. These acts issued in mental cruelty that resulted in periods of great mental distress such as is seen here in his words to the Corinthians Christians. Do not overlook Paul's premise. The same encouragement and comfort which he himself received from Christ is available to others. In this way still others would be encouraged and comforted by the same comfort with which they were comforted. All are to remember that the only real encouragement and consolation come from God through Jesus Christ, God's intermediate Agent. In this way the Corinthian Christians who composed a part of the body of Christ were to comfort one another with the abundant comfort each one had received from God in his own hours of trial.

In this verse one finds the very foundation of Christian doctrine and revelation, namely, the divine relationship that exists between the Christian and God the Father and our Lord Jesus Christ as the result of God's redemptive act. Paul's use of the word "comfort" is found frequently in the New Testament in the sense of "Divine Comfort" (see Luke 2:25; Acts 9:31; John 14:16).

> For just as the sufferings of Christ overflow into us, even so, through Jesus Christ, our consolation overflows (v. 5).

Here Paul saw an intermingling of the sufferings of Christ with the sufferings of His followers. From the moment Christ Jesus began His messianic mission, His enemies were determined and endeavored to put Him to death. Jesus lived under the death threat continually and that is why at times it was necessary for Him to avoid the multitudes (of which His adversaries were a part) so that His earthly mission would not be cut short. The sufferings of Christ actually overflow into the lives of those who are "in Christ." The relationship is that close. That is to say, the actual sufferings which Christ experienced are so "extended" as to be shared by His followers. Christ, of course, took on Himself sufferings that finally resulted in the sufferings of the cross wherein we have, as Paul developed it, the doctrine of atonement. These sufferings of Christ constitute the historical basis for our doctrine of the atonement made possible by Christ's death on the cross. The Christian must remember that he is to be a fellow sufferer with Christ. Such was the dream and the desire of the apostle Paul. Paul actually wanted to share in His sufferings (see Paul's words in Rom. 8:17; Phil. 3:10; Col. 1:24). In this fellowship of suffering there comes into the life of the believer consolation from the union in Christ (1 Pet. 4:13).

> But whether we are afflicted, it is in behalf of your encouragement and salvation; or whether we are comforted, it is in the interest of your encouragement which manifests itself in the patient endurance of the same sufferings which we ourselves are experiencing (v. 6).

Paul did not regard his suffering as any part of a substitute offering in behalf of the initial act of redemption but rather looked toward and helped to produce a much more effective "working out" of the human life-style that God expects of believers. It was merely a phase of Paul's influence and mission as a follower of Christ. Paul came to know more about Jesus and His intent for humanity and therefore lent himself more completely to the effective fruition of that intent. It is an energizing force that brings comfort and encouragement to the believer in Christ and makes for patient endurance of the sufferings whether mental or physical in the course of the Christian's daily witness. One sees here a divine blending of the two experiences—the experience of suffering and the experience of consolation—and they both come from God in the hour of need.

The difficulties that some expositors find in Paul's use of the word "salvation" *(sōtēria)* in relation to affliction is due, I believe, to a lack of understanding of the word *salvation*. There are three emphases of the word *salvation* in the Epistles of Paul. *One reference* has to do with the saving process that takes place immediately, by the grace of God, when one turns to Him in full and certain faith (Eph. 2:8-9). *A second aspect* has to do with the life-style of the Christian (Phil. 2:12). The believer is to grow constantly in his understanding of the purposes of God in Christ Jesus, and by so much his life-style is affected in the application of those truths. *The third emphasis* relates to the final outcome of one's salvation that takes place at "the last day" (Rom 13:11), whether at death or at the second coming of Christ.

> **And our hope concerning you is unchangeable, knowing that as you are sharers of our sufferings, so also are you of the consolation (v. 7).**

Here is revealed the deep insight of the apostle Paul concerning both his own afflictions and those of his fellow Christians: his trials brought comfort to them and taught them to make the most of their own relationship with Christ and with each other. There develops through suffering a common bond of fellowship in Christ. Each, in turn, makes for interpersonal sympathy. This makes it clear that the sufferings of the Corinthian Christians were to be no different from His own sufferings. Through such there comes to the believer steadfast endurance.

Apparently Paul had no special type of afflictions in mind but rather alludes to trouble in the sufferings and the consolations of Christ's followers. He makes it clear that suffering comes as a result of one's witness in behalf of Christ and also that divine consolation follows, even as was promised in the Great Commission (Matt. 28:19-20).

There is nothing here to indicate that Paul had a desire to motivate suffering *per se* on the part of the Corinthian Christians. His words were rather to be taken as an assurance that, whatever came to them in the way of trials, the great Helper would come to their cry of need. David Livingstone, the great English missionary, was quoted as saying to a group of students that if they would like to know what it was that sustained him in his long journeys in Africa, marked by many trials, it was in his consciousness of the Great Commission of Jesus in which He promised to be with His witnesses "until the end of the world" (Matt. 28:19-20). But Paul's hope was unshaken by the trials and tribulations that came upon him and would eventually come upon others. He realized that in being partakers of Christ's suffering one is also a partaker of His consolation and encouragement.

Paul had spoken of the divine comfort that comes to the followers of Christ in sufferings and of the encouragement of others which also seems to make for steadfast faith on the part of those who witness. Now there comes a change of emphasis in his dialogue.

(2) For God's Deliverance (vv. 8-10)

Certainly we do not want you to be ignorant, brothers, concerning our affliction that took place in Asia, that we were burdened altogether beyond our strength, so that we despaired even of life, but we ourselves have had within ourselves the sentence of death, that we should not trust in ourselves but in God, who raises the dead; who delivered us from so great a death, and will continue to deliver us; in whom we have set our hope that He will keep on delivering us in the future.

For a better understanding of the motive of this experience, turn and read again verse 6. Where did the experience take place? Very likely it occurred in Ephesus, for there were many adversaries there (1 Cor. 15:32; 16:9). Wherever it took place, it must have been very severe, for Paul was not one to wince at small confrontations which he encountered on his pilgrimage. He was one who could say, "I am able for anything in Him who fills me with power" (Phil. 4:13). But wherever his tribulation took place, and whatever its character, the Corinthians must have known about it. Of course the trial could have been that of grave physical illness which brought him near death's door. In the dramatic emphasis on the all but overwhelming experience of Paul and his sufferings, the word to "despair," seldom found in the Bible, and the "burden" pictured here resemble that of "an overladen ship" (Chrysostom). Certainly only those who have dwelt for a season at the gate of death fully comprehend Paul's words here. But whatever, whenever, and wherever the overburdening experience of life comes to the Christian, he has the assurance that God, who works with him, "is trustworthy" and is able to deliver him completely from natural harassment and even death itself. In this truth there is no ambiguity. He is no "Yes" and "No." Sidney Barrett states it well: "God's promises are plainly intelligible, and what He promises, He performs. There is no fickleness about Him."

(3) For Prayer Help (v. 11)

Also you help by joining in prayer for us, so that the favor which you do may be bestowed upon us through the prayers of many people.

This is the verse that has given translators difficulty because of Paul's use of the word *prosōpon* and the double use of the word *pollōn*. Now the word *prosōpon* originally stood for the face, countenance, as "before the face of Christ" (2 Cor. 2:10). The word was also used in the ancient writings to convey the idea of *person*. This seems to be the general idea of Paul in verse 11 where the Corinthians pray for him (1:11a), and he may have in mind here the prayers of other Christians in his behalf. This would hardly be foreign to Paul's accustomed way of reckoning the support of fellow Christians far and wide in a time of crisis. At any rate, there is a beautiful figure here of the cooperation of Christians in their prayer life on behalf of their spiritual leaders. Paul was indeed a man of prayer. He could not have been otherwise with this deep understanding of the prayer life of Jesus who, on at least one occasion, spent a whole night, alone, in prayer before the choice of the twelve. There were those who did pray for Paul and support his ministry with love and with prayer. And this we think is the idea here—the cooperation of Christians in their support of him. What would happen in churches today if the spiritual leaders had the assurance that the people to whom they minister were constantly holding them up in prayer to God? The effect of such prayerful support would likely be beyond measure. The word "favor" which Paul used here is an untranslated Greek word which gives us our English word *charisma*. And that is what a prayer amounts to in the lives of believers—it is a charismatic experience that may be imparted to other believers employed in holiness and purity. When the prayers of "many people" cooperate toward a given cause that is right in the sight of God, the result can only be glorious.

2 CORINTHIANS 2

¹But I decided this, in my own mind, not to come to you again in sorrow;

²for if I make you be sorrowful, who then makes me glad but the one made sad by me?

³And I wrote this very thing lest in coming to you I might have sorrow from them from whom I ought to rejoice, having confidence in you all that my joy is *the joy* of you all.

⁴For out of much distress and anguish of heart, I wrote to you through many tears, not that you might become sad, but that you might come to know all the more the love which I have for you.

⁵But if anyone has caused sorrow, he did it not to me alone, but to some extent that I might not deal too severely with you all.

⁶Sufficient for such a person is this reproach delivered *to him* by the many.

⁷Instead of punishing him, you should forgive him and encourage him, lest by any means such a person should be overwhelmed by the greater sorrow.

⁸This is why I beg you urgently to confirm your love for him;

⁹for to this end also I wrote that I might come to know your character, whether you are obedient in all things.

¹⁰For to whom you forgive anything, I also *forgive;* for what I also have forgiven, if I have forgiven anything, *it is* for your sakes in the presence of Christ,

¹¹that we may not be taken advantage of by Satan, for we are not ignorant of his designs.

¹²Now when I came to Troas in order *to preach* the Gospel of Christ, although a door was opened for me in the Lord,

¹³I got no rest for my spirit since I did not find Titus, my brother; consequently I said goodbye to them and left for Macedonia.

¹⁴But thanks be to God, who always leads us in triumph in the Christ and makes manifest through us the fragrance of Christ unto God

¹⁵among those who are being saved and among them who are perishing,

¹⁶to the latter the odor of death unto death, but to the former the fragrance of life unto life. And who is qualified for these things?

¹⁷for we are not like the majority who are peddling the Word of God; rather as from pure motives, we speak as from God before God in Christ.

2

Paul and His Current Travel Plans

2 Corinthians 1:12 to 2:4

1. His Obvious Sincerity (vv. 12-14)

For our boasting is this: the testimony of our consciousness, that it is in the holiness and purity of God, not in fleshly wisdom but in the grace of God, we conducted ourselves in the world, and all the more toward you (v. 12).

The word "boasting" used here by Paul was a word used variously in the New Testament, as of pride one has in someone (2 Cor. 7:4). It is used also in the sense of exultation, glorying. Paul's use of the word here goes much further than "bragging." Paul told us the cause of his boasting. He had the support of his conscience, a conscience marked by the holiness and purity of God. His purity was not based on fleshly wisdom or on carnal man. The mere conscience of man is not enough in itself to direct an individual in just and upright conduct. For a conscience to have spiritual validity it must be a conscience that has its origin in and is developed by God, not by man.

The word "purity," often translated "sincerity," calls for more than sincerity. A person may be completely sincere, on the basis of his own conscience, and yet be far away from the holiness and purity of God. Who is there to say, for instance, that all of our forefathers who engaged in the awful practice of human slavery were not sincere? The sincerity of the heart in no way justifies the action of the hands and the head. Paul's words to the Corinthians about his life-style were a simple declaration that his life was lived without reproach in holiness and morality. And he endeavored all

27

the more to achieve such a life-style, in view of his Corinthian friends in Christ.

Could it be at this point that contemporary Christians manifest one of their greatest weaknesses? Is the average follower of Christ careful enough about the cultivation of his conscience to the end that it may lead to a God kind of holiness and purity? Herein is the true foundation of all graceful, noble, interpersonal relationships. If people strive faithfully to implement in their own lives the full intent of the Father's will as it relates to self, to substance, and to others, there can be little opportunity for the traumatic experiences of life that occur so often in the lives of Christians in their regard for one another. Fleshly wisdom takes no account of spiritual things, and neither does worldly wisdom. The words "in the grace of God" mean that Paul's conscience and his life-style were the result of the manifestation of God's redemptive love in his own life. He had an experience in that redemptive love to such a remarkable degree that it turned his life completely around on the Damascus road, and in such a decisive and final manner that he never returned to his old life-style that had made him the enemy of the church and of the followers of Christ.

The Christian conscience is a powerful factor in the life of a godly man. But a conscience, to be Christian, must be constantly edified by Christian concepts of truth and duty.

> **For we are not writing anything to you other than what you read and understand, and I hope you will continue to understand to the end (v. 13).**

Paul wanted the Corinthians to realize that there was no "hidden meaning in his letters" (Bernard). But it would be difficult for one to perceive Paul engaging in "double talk." He spoke in a clear and articulate manner when dealing with even the most sensitive issues. Paul was bold in his utterances and beyond reproach. It is a painful thing for a spiritual leader to be misunderstood when his purposes are pure and upright and where his intentions are holy. Certainly Paul was sincere and straightforward at all times in his dialogue with his fellow Christians. Nevertheless, the Corinthians apparently questioned the sincerity of his intentions. The fact that Paul did not go directly to the

Corinthians on the intended visit was in no way due to failure of desire but rather to the circumstances that caused him to postpone his anticipated visit with them.

> **And just as you did partially understand us that, even as we are your glorying, you are also ours in the day of our Lord Jesus (v. 14).**

Paul here portrayed a beautiful expression of the mutual joy that comes to the witness and to those who receive the witness; there is a reciprocal relationship, a joyful reciprocity, that is uniquely glorious. The triumphant feeling expressed here is a contrast to the apologetic mood expressed in verses 15 and 16. His single-mindedness and integrity could hardly have been made more manifest than in these unselfish words of praise of his fellow Christians. Obviously there is no trace of any feeling of superiority on his part with reference to the cause of the glorying. There is utterly no place in the community relationships of Christians for the "big I" and "little you." Christians are rather in honor to prefer one another, to give place to one another, to subordinate themselves in their own eyes in relationship to others. If, of course, the Christian is marked by meekness and humility, there can be no problem in this respect. The overemphasis on place and the personal desire for eminence and praise serve to denigrate the divine intent with reference to all personal relationships of Christians.

2. His Change of Plans (1:15 to 2:4)

> **And with this confidence, I decided to come to you earlier, that you might have a second favor, and to pass through you to Macedonia, and again from Macedonia to come to you, and by you to be helped on my journey to Judea (vv. 15-16).**

Apparently Paul had planned earlier to cross the Aegean Sea to Corinth, and then go to Macedonia from which he would later journey by way of Corinth unto Judea, taking along the contributions of the Corinthian Christians in behalf of the poor saints in Jerusalem (1 Cor. 16:3-4). In 1 Corinthians 5:9 there is a reference to a letter that was lost. It is possible that Paul had communicated his travel plans to the Corinthian church in the lost letter; but, when the bad news reached Paul concerning the conditions in the Corinthian church, he changed his plans to bypass Corinth en route to Macedonia and to visit with them on his way to Judea. It was this change of plans that evidently prompted the reproach of the Corinthians (1:17). So Paul rose to his own defense in behalf of the decisions he had made. Maybe Paul did not want to see the Corinthians face-to-face until some time had passed following his first letter in which he had taken the Corinthians to task in regard to the bad news that had come to his ear. On the other hand, Paul might have changed his travel plans for purposes all his own. Paul did not go into detail (v. 16) concerning the "help" that he anticipated from the Corinthians to aid him on his journey to Judea, but Herring suggests that he might have had in mind delegates from Corinth to accompany him to Judea. At any rate, Paul had in heart the moral and spiritual welfare of the Corinthian saints and took the course that he did in altering his travel plans in what he considered the best interests of the Corinthians. Certainly Paul contemplated help on the part of the Corinthians, and such was not unusual. Fellow Christians were accustomed to rendering aid and "seeing off" their visiting evangelists on their further missions.

> **In making this decision, therefore, did I consequently act in fickleness? Or the plans I make, do I make them according to the flesh, that there should be with me the Yes, Yes and the No, No? (v. 17).**

Some think that Paul's words here may refer to Matthew 5:37 and James 5:12. But whether they do or not, one thing is obvious: Paul changed his mind about the time of the proposed visit. It also seems that this is the matter that sparked the criticism of his adversaries and led them to infer that he was a fickle type of person in making plans and changing them for personal or selfish reasons. All we know about the life of the apostle Paul would refute any idea of selfishness on his part. He was a man who undertook to carry out in full the Father's purpose. It would seem that, from the day of his Damascus experience when he met Jesus face to face, his one desire was expressed in the words,

"What wilt Thou have me to do?" (Acts 9:6). This desire carried him to the street called Straight in Damascus and thence to his full-time life service among the Gentiles as a witness to the gospel of Christ.

But since God is faithful, our word to you is not an ambiguous Yes and No (v. 18).

Here again Paul defended himself against the charge of ambiguity. There can hardly be found a trace of such in his life when one looks at the cold, hard facts of his day-by-day witnessing from the beginning to the very end of his days. One can hardly read the account of his travels and his response to the call of duty without a feeling that he lived in the sense of that call in earnest endeavor to carry out the purposes of Christ daily. "For I am already being offered up, and the time of my departure is at hand; I have fought the good fight, I have finished the course, I have kept the faith" (2 Tim. 4:7-8). Surely Paul's example should impress the contemporary servants of Christ of the necessity to rid themselves of any measure of ambiguity. Indeed, this should give the young enrollees for special training in our theological seminaries food for thought. Should they not, at the time of their enrollment, have a clear-cut idea or vision as to the character of their future labors? Again and again, one hears the words, "I don't know at this time that my calling is to be minister of the gospel in the sense that I would pastor a church, but I feel that it relates to some area of Christian witness." Would it not seem reasonable to believe that God is able to guide and give an understandable directive in relation to the future course of the young man and the young woman's life work before they enter institutions for special training? If God is calling one to be a preacher of the gospel, or to serve in another area of Christian witness, is there room to doubt that God will make the nature of the calling clear if the prospective leader will only acquaint himself with the fields of service in which he may serve, and then fall upon his knees and tarry in prayer—maybe all night long, as Jesus tarried on at least one occasion? Let no one dwell in an ambiguous mood for long. Let the contemporary young "Timothy" find his task under God and then let him bend all his energies, day and night, in preparation for that given task. Time is too precious to be wasted in ambiguity.

> **For God's Son, Jesus Christ, who was proclaimed among you through us, through me and Silvanus and Timothy, was not an ambiguous Yes and No, but rather in Him was the Yes (v. 19).**

Paul made it clear that Christ Jesus is to be the core of the proclamation and in Him there is no trace of equivocation in any of His words or deeds. In fact, the final "Yes" came to be pronounced in Him. The witness is to be concerned with carrying out God's "Yes" that at times may call for a change of plans, as was true in Paul's case, and the change may call for a "No" in the eyes of man.

Upon his arrival in Corinth (Acts 18:1-4), Paul was alone but was later joined by Silas and Timothy (v. 5), who shared in his effort among the Corinthians. He had obviously begun his mission alone, however, and this is why he doubtless reverted to the singular use of the personal pronoun ("through me"). But the message of Paul and Timothy and Silvanus was the same. They preached the same gospel, and this gospel was Christ. God's "Yes" is not influenced by man's desires. It is an affirmation of God's will, of God's desire. Saying "Yes" to God may come to mean "saying 'No' to man." In Jesus Christ, God's eternal "Yes" came to be (Bernard). Paul's dialogue here confirmed his own concept of the unchangeableness of God.

3. The Promises of God (v. 20)

> **For, as many as are the promises of God, in Him is the Yes; therefore, through Him also is the Amen to God, unto His glory through us.**

This verse, called by many a difficult verse, seems to me to be an affirmation of all that has been said in verses 18 and 19. Jesus Christ is simply the fulfillment of all the promises of God as they relate to the redemption of sinful people. In Him is God's eternal "Yes." God the Father is the guarantor witness and minister of

Christ Himself as both the fulfillment and the confirmation of God's promises. No matter how many promises God made, their supreme affirmation is Christ, and that affirmation constitutes in itself an "Amen" to the reality of God's promises. Among Christian congregations in this first century, it was customary for the people to say "Amen" at the end of prayers. This "Amen" amounted to an affirmation of the content of the prayer. Here the Christians are participants in this affirmation. Their witness, by means of their testimony and the integrity of their lives, as well as their responses to the commandments of God, abound to God's glory. God's faithfulness to His people is communicated by Himself. He motivated and made possible solidity and steadfastness on the part of Paul and the Corinthians.

Paul's words to us are indeed significant for persons of every age. We are God's ambassadors. We are His instrument of approach to the ills of society that afflict our land. And herein lies more than the shadow of the cross of the Christian. The Christian's cross is his effort to share the burden of Christ's redemptive love for the world. And whatever the failure, the Christian feels the divine responsibility projected initially by Christ in His effort to redeem that lost world; then as he responds to that consciousness whereby he feels the burden that Jesus felt, entering into the human side of the redemptive process, by so much he finds his cross.

The fact that the average Christian does not have that sense of burden is clearly manifested in the response of church members in the stewardship of their talents and their substance in the furtherance of Christ's mission on earth. The financial burden of the church rests on the shoulders of approximately one third of the members of the average church. Is not this in itself a woeful indictment of the character of the confession of church members by and large? Whatever the response of the Christians to the promises of God, it is to be unto the glory of God.

4. The Seal of the Holy Spirit (vv. 21-22)

Now he that keeps on strengthening us together with you in Christ, and has anointed us, is God, who also has marked us

with His seal and given us the first installment of the Spirit in our hearts.

In these two verses one comes to the heart of the Christian revelation in its relation to the individual believer. God not only guarantees His promises and the effective relationship of those promises, but He also anoints, seals, and gives the Christian the first installment of the promised blessings that he will realize in full at the last day.

The use of the seal in ancient writings served as proof that no one had tampered with the document or goods in question. It was evidence that the document had not been falsified. This commercial term therefore was employed by Paul to illustrate the faithfulness of God in His relationship to His children. The seal indicates that the Christian belongs to Him and is therefore "secured ready to meet examination at the day of judgment" (Barrett, p. 79) (see Ezek. 9:4). Notice also that this pledge *(arrabōna)* of the Spirit was given *in the heart* of the believer and that the pledge consists of the Spirit, the divine agent of Christ. By the Spirit the believer is given undeniable assurance of his continuing relationship with Christ, a relationship that he will experience in its full measure at the last day.

It is not difficult to see the Trinitarian implications of verses 21-22—God the Father, Christ the Son, and the Holy Spirit all work together in projecting God's redemptive purpose in behalf of the lost world. And the Christian himself becomes a part of the "Amen" in giving of the glory to God (vv. 21-22).

5. Co-Workers (vv. 23-24)

And I call upon God as a witness against my soul that, intentionally sparing you, I came not again to Corinth (v. 23).

Paul revealed clearly his reason for the delay of his plans to visit Corinth. He desired that there would be ample time for the meaning of his first letter to reach their hearts. He wanted his visit not to take away from his former message to them, and his next visit to be less painful. It was really his desire to "spare" them that caused him to change his plans to arrive at a later time. Paul's words reveal his tender spirit and his deep regard for the Corin thians as they responded to the challenge of his first letter. It also reveals his patience and his hopes for a favorable response on the part of the Corinthians to his spirited challenge.

> **It is not that we are lording it over your faith, but that we are co-workers for your joy; for it is by your faith that you stand (v. 24).**

Paul had no disposition to have dominion over the faith of the Corinthians. He was not a tyrant and he did not want them to look upon him as such. He desired rather that they think of him as a fellow worker—their joy. The "we" here could refer to the joint efforts of Paul, Silvanus, and Timothy. On the other hand, Paul may be speaking just for himself. Paul in no way complimented the character of the faith of the Corinthians, but he did want to help the immature Christians develop the Christian stature God intended for them to have and to experience God's intended joy for them. This parenthetical statement in verse 24 appears to be an added effort to guard against misunderstanding on the part of the Corinthians. Paul wanted them to realize that by their own faith they would stand. Indeed, the character of one's faith is determinative. It is seen in every word and every deed of the Christian's life. Paul's fondest hope for the Corinthian Christians was that they might become mature both in their understanding of Christ's will for their lives and in their daily application of Christian truth in their lives.

In 2 Corinthians 2, Paul sounded much like a pastor speaking to his own congregation. Of course his relationship with the Corinthian church had come to be sentimental, and the bonds of friendship close, or he would hardly have been able to speak to them in his first letter (1 Cor.) as he did, with stinging words of rebuke. But Paul had sown the seeds of Christian truth in the hearts of the Corinthian believers and he wanted the disciples to grow up and become mature in their thinking and acting and to be in accord with the mind and life-style of Jesus. His relationship with the Corinthian church was strong, for his own strength, as Tennyson once said, "Is as the strength of ten," because his heart was pure, and his motives in all of his relationship with the church were marked by integrity of mind and heart and deed. There was nothing in his words and deeds that reflected compromise of his Christian truth as he had come to see it in his relationship with Jesus and the Word.

6. A Personal Decision (2:1-2)

> **But I decided this, in my own mind, not to come to you again in sorrow; for if I make you be sorrowful, who then makes me glad but the one made sad by me?**

No outside pressure created the motive for Paul's decision to delay his subsequent visit to Corinth. He made up his own mind, irrespective of past events and present circumstances. Paul had been bold and unrelenting in his admonitions to them in his first letter, and his words were obviously stern in their rebuke of those who were departing from the Christian life-style under the influence of heathen customs. The point is that Paul did not want to open up old wounds and further aggravate their dispositions toward him and the truth that he had sought so earnestly to make clear to them, by paying a fresh visit before the truth had taken hold of their minds and they had come to themselves in their understanding of his message to them. The situation, at best, was an unhappy one, and it would take time for healing to come. Dr. John A. Broadus was quoted by one of his students as saying that, when it is necessary for a pastor to denounce or severely flay members of his flock, he should be sure that the words of rebuke are followed by words that make for healing and understanding. In other words, when a person has been cast down by words of denunciation, he should not be left lying in his misery, but lifted up with words of hope and healing. Whatever the words of punishment might be for misconduct, or disorder, the discipline should lead to understanding and hope. Paul's words "come again to you in sorrow" surely suggest a previous visit, not the original visit which issued in the founding of the Corinthian church, but a later visit. This could indicate that Paul had visited Corinth at least twice before the writing of this epistle (12:14;

13:1f.). It is obvious, however, that in this previous visit there was
sorrow in his heart because of the state of things he found, and
he did not want to come to them again "in sorrow," therefore he
made up his own mind not to do so.

At any rate, the second visit of Paul to Corinth must have fallen
between the writing of First and Second Corinthians. (See 1 Cor.
16:5ff. for a reference to Paul's intended visit to Corinth.) Originally Paul had not made the promised visit to the Corinthian
church at the expected time. Of course there was *pain* for Paul in
either course he would choose to take. But at least by delaying
the visit for a while, the intensity of the misunderstandings and of
the disposition not to heed his words of admonition might sub-
side until the Corinthians would receive him more readily. Paul's
words in verse 3 explain clearly his motive in deferring the promised visit.

7. Paul's Love for the Corinthians (vv. 3-4)

> **And I wrote this very thing lest in coming to you I might have
> sorrow from them from whom I ought to rejoice, having con-
> fidence in you all that my joy is *the joy* of you all (v. 3).**

A delicate sense of "balance" and "imbalance" is reflected here
in Paul's closing words in verse 3. In other words, there is a mutual dependence, an interdependence, between Paul and the
Corinthian Christians so far as Christian happiness is concerned.
He said in effect, "Your joy is my joy, and my joy is yours." At
least Paul did not wish to increase the bitterness and severity of
his caustic words of reproof. He wanted healing and restoration
of the Christian life-style on the part of all of the members of the
church. The point should be made here, however, that there is
nothing to suggest that Paul's words of reproof were intended for
all of the members of the church at Corinth. His overall statement
of the matter certainly leads one to assume that there was indeed
a loyal group of the Christians who must have received his words
in the right spirit. Paul's words in verse 4 reflect the emotional
distress of his own heart in writing his letter which gave to the
Corinthians in unmistakable terms his words of reproof:

> For out of much distress and anguish of heart, I wrote to you
> through many tears, not that you might become sad, but
> that you might come to know all the more the love which I
> have for you (v. 4).

His purpose in writing was not to make the offenders sad, but
to let them know the love which he had for them. The word *love*
which Paul used here *(agapēn)* refers to love in its purest, highest
form—the love which God expressed for the lost world in send-
ing His Son to be the Savior and the love which the believer has
in his heart for God and for his fellowman as he manifests, in
interpersonal relationships, the character of this divine love. Certainly Paul made clear "the assurance of his affection" for the
Corinthians. Animated as his message was by the love of God,
he really did not want the Corinthians to remain in any mood of
sadness and grief.

8. His Forgiving Spirit (2:5-11)

In verse 5 Paul furnished added insight concerning the root of
the trouble that had brought about unhappiness:

> But if anyone has caused sorrow, he did it not to me alone,
> but to some extent that I might not deal too severely with you
> all.

To whom does Paul refer in this passage? Who was the offender? Some think he was a stranger, but this is hardly compati-
ble with Paul's words in verse 6, for a stranger would hardly have
been subject to punishment by the church. And what was the
character of the offense? Here again there is difficulty. Certainly
the passage does not appear to relate to the offender in
1 Corinthians 5:1. It could be that some member or group of the
Corinthian Christians had taken issue with Paul by challenging
his right to deal with them as he had dealt. But Paul clearly answered any such question in 1:24: "Not that we are lording it
over your faith, but that we are co-workers for your joy. . . ."

If there had been an insult, it might have been in such measure, or in such a way, as to offend the whole community of
believers; but Paul treaded lightly on the matter and did not want

to increase the tension brought about by the incident. Hence his words, "that I might not deal too severely" (2:5b). In verses 6 and 7 we find Paul in the role of the mediator in its high and beautiful expression, so far as human relations are concerned.

Sufficient for such a person in this reproach delivered *to him* by the many (v. 6).

Whatever action the congregation may have taken in the matter was over and the time had come for reconciliation. Paul's words do not define the character of the offense, nor that of the action taken by the congregation, but the words "by the many" suggest that the majority of the congregation approved of the action taken. But whatever the punishment was, Paul regarded it as sufficient (v. 6) and thought that the time had come for forgiveness, for restoration, and for encouragement:

Instead of punishing him, you should forgive him and encourage him, lest by any means such a person should be overwhelmed by the greater sorrow (v. 7).

Sometimes there is a disposition, on the part of some, to "rub salt" into a wound, and such can only make the situation far worse for the offender. Occasionally one hears an expression like this: "He not only told him off, but rubbed it in!" Certainly Paul said that whatever action the church had taken, and the response of the offender, it was such as to call for the future of love and merciful hope toward the offender. Such is the only course that the Christian should take toward an offending brother. Any other course may serve to inflict an excoriating wound in his own heart and to denigrate his own motives.

When a person is cast down by his own misdeeds, and is conscious of the fact that what he has done is seen as wrong not only in the eyes of God, but also in the eyes of his fellowman, he is in a state of need for repentance, forgiveness, and encouragement. At times the spirit of forgiveness may call for a manifestation on the part of the offended person even when there is no overt request for such on the part of the offender. A young minister, in preparation for his life's work at a seminary, tells this story: "I became greatly offended by one of my peers who criticized me in a derogatory manner and spoke damagingly of my purpose in life. The root of his complaint, I later found out, was that he felt my sole interest, during the days of study, was making grades. He felt that I had little time for others. As I thought on the chafing remarks that he had made about me, I felt myself avoiding him. I didn't want to see him, and I didn't want to spend any time with him. The thing began to act on my heart as gangrene. Finally, when I could not bear to put up with the situation in my own heart any longer, I went to the offender, whom I found shoveling coal in the boiler room of the basement heating system, and said to him: 'I have come to tell you that the remarks you made about me, many days ago, offended me and that I can no longer live with the lack of peace in my heart and the kind of feelings I have had toward you. I have come to tell you that I forgive you and I want you as my friend, and I want to be your friend.' The offender took hold of my hand and led me as we climbed the iron stairway to the room above where there was the desired privacy, and we knelt there in earnest prayer. Of course there was instant forgiveness on both sides, and the two of us became lasting friends."

Paul did not tell us what happened to the offender after his encouragement to manifest love toward him. But one can only surmise, even though evidence is lacking, that the ending was a happy one for the offender and for Paul and the Corinthian church. And we no longer wonder that Paul said in the closing words of 1 Corinthians 13, "And now abide faith, hope, love, these three; but the greatest of these is love" (v. 13).

Paul brought to a close his dialogue on this subject with the words:

> **This is why I beg you urgently to confirm your love for him; for to this end also I wrote that I might come to know your character, whether you are obedient in all things (vv. 8-9).**

Paul may have surprised the Corinthian Christians upon his admission to them that he wanted to have an opportunity to know them more fully and the character of their obedience to Christ. The American Standard Version has, "that I might know the proof of you." The language Paul used in verse 9 means literally "the proof of you in the matter of obedience." It hardly seems likely that Paul had in mind here obedience to him or to his apostleship, though the scope of meaning might include that. For what Paul spoke to the Corinthians, he spoke "in Christ," and such teachings as he gave them were divinely inspired. Of course there was represented in Paul the authority of Christ, as he related to the mind and the will of Christ. Paul made it clear that he was looking for full obedience, not partial as one finds today in the life-style of so many professing believers in Christ. And it is at this point that one comes to the much offending on the part of members of churches today. They are not "obedient in all things." If one is to consider the affirmation of Jesus, "by their fruits ye shall know them," does verse 10 imply that the church had already acted in forgiveness of the misdeed by the erring brother? If so, Paul declared his own support of the action. Here is what he said:

> **For to whom you forgive anything, I also *forgive;* for what I also have forgiven, if I have forgiven anything, *it is* for your sakes in the presence of Christ (v. 10).**

Certainly Paul's position concerning the forgiveness of the erring brother was not taken merely to dispose "of an awkward situation" and placate an enemy (Barrett). Here as elsewhere in his relationship with the Corinthians, he had at heart the welfare of the Corinthian church, and in doing so, he called Christ to witness to his position. In Paul's reference to Satan, he used an old word which means "to take advantage of, to cheat, to outwit, to defraud"; and there could hardly be a more apt description of the ways of Satan. Paul went on to interpret the action of God's forgiveness of the offender by saying,

> **that we may not be taken advantage of by Satan, for we are not ignorant of his designs (v. 11).**

The situation afforded Paul an excellent opportunity to awaken Christians to the devices of Satan which, even in the life of churches today, are used to wreck churches by dividing the membership into opposing groups and, by so much, plunging the body of believers into a state of spiritual inertia.

9. His Journey to Macedonia (2:12-13)

The scene now shifts to Troas, and Paul gave his reason for the journey there:

> Now when I came to Troas in order *to preach* the Gospel of Christ, although a door was opened for me in the Lord, I got no rest for my spirit since I did not find Titus, my brother; consequently I said goodbye to them and left for Macedonia.

Such was the motivating factor in all of Paul's missionary journeys. They were for the sake of the gospel of Christ. The name of Titus does not appear in Acts, but we find it again in Galatians 2:1,3 and again in 2 Timothy 4:10. Although Titus was a Gentile, Paul did not have him circumcised (Gal. 2:3), but there was evidently a very close tie between them as brothers in Christ. It appears that there were plans for him and Titus to meet in Troas, but obviously the plans did not mature. When Paul and Barnabas went from Antioch to Jerusalem for the conference there to settle the question concerning the necessity of circumcision for the Gentiles, Titus accompanied them (see Acts 15:2). (For general biographical notes on Titus, one must rely upon 2 Corinthians, Galatians, 2 Timothy, and Titus.) Apparently the evangelistic opportunity for Paul in Troas was not all that he desired. But a minister cannot enter every door of opportunity that opens for him. For instance, a minister tells the story of having two pulpit committees from two states present at the morning worship hour to hear him preach, and both of the committees wanted to elicit his concern for the opportunity their pulpits would offer him. The pastor met with the committees separately, neither committee having the knowledge of the other's presence. But when the day was over and there had been time for prayer, the pastor concluded that he could not enter either of the doors that apparently were opening wide to receive him. When a pastor leaves one field, where there is an open door, and moves on to another location, he should have his own consciousness of the leadership of the Lord and the certain peace that follows when one is completely guided by the Spirit of God in all pastoral moves. Certainly Paul found no rest for his soul in Troas when he did not find his brother Titus there; and for reasons known to him

and the Lord, he said good-bye to his friends at Troas and moved
on to Macedonia.

The Ministry of the New Covenant (2 Cor. 2:14 to 7:1)

1. The Triumphant Leadership of God in Christ (2:14-17)

Paul sounded a triumphant note in verses 14-16 saying,

> But thanks be to God, who always leads us in triumph in the
> Christ and makes manifest through us the fragrance of
> Christ unto God among those who are being saved and
> among them who are perishing, to the latter the odor of
> death unto death, but to the former the fragrance of life unto
> life. And who is qualified for these things?

The word translated "fragrance" is an old word used in the
days of Paul for a pleasant odor as that of ointment. But the same
word was used also of an unpleasant odor—hence, Paul's double use of the word here. To believers the knowledge of Christ
is as a "fragrance," a "pleasant odor." The expression "odor of
knowledge" or "fragrance of knowledge" is found in "The Wisdom Literature" (compare Ecclesiasticus 24:15; 39:14). But the
fragrance of the knowledge of God in Christ means one thing to
the believer and another thing to the unbeliever. To one it is a
"pleasant odor," whereas to the other (the unbeliever) it is as the
stench "of death" that leads to death. This is precisely the way
that hearers react to the gospel of Christ. To the saved, such
knowledge is sweeter than honey, even "the drippings of the
honeycomb." But to those whose minds and hearts are turned
away from God, the persuasive appealing words of the gospel
become a thing of disdain and of hateful disregard. In answer to
Paul's question, "And who is qualified for these things?" one
might say, "We are, and so is every minister of the Word who is
called of God, who has committed his life as a living sacrifice
unto God, and who is guided by Christ in all his words and in all
his ways."

Some have found difficulty in Paul's words, "who are being
saved" and "who are perishing" (v. 15). They regarded "neither
salvation nor perdition" as completed facts. But the participles
used by Paul hardly suppose such an emphasis. People were

being saved from day to day, we take it, in Corinth, as we would use the term in speaking of contemporary evangelism. After all, as the believer yields his heart to Christ he is "being saved," but salvation actually becomes a completed fact; and the believer accepts that fact. On the basis of the promises of God, he knows that it is "by grace" that salvation comes "through faith" and that it is "not of works," not of self, lest those saved should boast (Eph. 2:8-9). In the case of the perishing, however, the perishing is not a "completed fact" until death comes; and in a sense the lost person can at any time, while there is life, turn to the Savior and experience the "completed fact" of salvation. When a person is saved, he enters into a saved relationship with the Heavenly Father, a relationship which nothing in life can sever. Of course, in the saved relationship he is to grow in grace and in knowledge and in the application of Christian truth in his daily life-style. What is more, the ultimate joys of the saved experience come at the last day. In verse 17, Paul has these arresting words:

> **For we are not like the majority who are peddling the Word of God; rather as from pure motives, we speak as from God before God in Christ.**

Paul said here, in substance, "We are not spiritual hucksters, peddling our wares with wrong motives." But Paul is not to be regarded here as complimenting himself unduly and his fellow proclaimers of the gospel. It was an established fact that there were many who were "watering down" the gospel of Christ and who had ulterior motives in their proclamation. From the word translated "the majority," we get our English word *hoi polloi*, meaning the common people, the masses, and that is the word Paul used here as he applied it to those who were "peddling" the Word of God. The word "peddling" is from an old word meaning to "trade in," "huckster," "peddle"; in some instances it touches the meaning of *adulterate*. Paul declared that his motives were pure and that he spoke "as from God" and "before God." He did not hesitate to call Christ as witness and God as witness to his motive and message. But there are to be found, here and there, counterfeit preachers just as in the days of Paul. This is indeed a lamentable fact, but one of which all are made aware, now and then, in contemporary records of pastors and church members. How else is one to regard the preacher who has, if only occasionally, his mistress on the side, in abject betrayal of his marriage vows and his vows of presentation to God as a preacher of His Word?

2 CORINTHIANS 3

¹Are we starting again to commend ourselves? or do we need (as some do) letters of commendation to you or from you?

²You are our letter written in our hearts, known and read by all men;

³for you are becoming known as an epistle of Christ, cared for by us, written not with ink but with the Spirit of the Living God, not on tablets of stone but on heart tablets of flesh.

⁴For we have such self-confidence through Christ toward God.

⁵Not that we are qualified, of ourselves, to take credit for anything, as from ourselves, for our capability is from God,

⁶who has qualified us (rendered us fit) to be servants of the new covenant, not of the letter but of the Spirit; for the letter kills but the Spirit gives life.

⁷Now if the ministry of death engraved in letters on stones came into existence in glory, so that the children of Israel could not look intently into the face of Moses on account of the glory of his face, glory that was passing away,

⁸how much more in glory will be the ministry of the Spirit?

⁹For if there was glory in the ministry of the condemnation, by much more does the ministry of righteousness abound in glory;

¹⁰for that which has been made glorious has not been made glorious, in this respect, on account of the surpassing glory (of the New Covenant).

¹¹For if that which passes away was through glory, by how much more that which remains is in glory.

¹²Having therefore a hope such as this, we act with great boldness in speech,

¹³and not as Moses did who put a veil upon his face so the children of Israel should not look intently into the conclusion of that which was passing away.

¹⁴But their minds became hardened, and for this reason unto this day the same veil that in Christ is abolished remains unlifted in the public reading of the old covenant.

¹⁵Accordingly until this day when Moses is read, a veil lies upon their hearts.

¹⁶But whenever it shall turn to the Lord the veil is taken away.

¹⁷Now the Lord is the Spirit; and where the Spirit of the Lord is, *there is* freedom.

¹⁸But we all with unveiled face keep on reflecting, as in a mirror, the glory of the Lord, being transformed into the same likeness, from glory unto glory, just as from the Spirit of the Lord.

3

The New Covenant Relationship

2 Corinthians 3:1-18

Before continuing his stirring dialogue concerning the ministry of the new covenant, in contrast to the old, Paul used the occasion as an opportunity to further his defense of his own ministry and to scout the idea, as far as he was concerned, of the need of any letters of commendation. The use of such letters was widespread in the secular communities in Paul's day. It was also common practice in the Christian community. Paul did commend Titus and his companion, for instance, in this epistle (8:22ff.). He commended Phoebe, a Christian "in the imperial capital" (Rom. 16:1); so Paul in no wise intended to denigrate such letters of commendation, but only to affirm the fact that he had no need of them in behalf of himself. But since false prophets had infiltrated the fellowship of the Christians in Corinth, Paul's remarks were all the more fitting.

(1) An Epistle of Christ (vv. 1-3)

Are we starting again to commend ourselves? or do we need (as some do) letters of commendation to you or from you (v. 1)?

Who were the "some" to whom Paul referred? Perhaps they were the false brethren who had come into the community of believers with a view to stirring up trouble. It is easy for one who has close friends to receive from them letters of commendation. Even the most unworthy may succeed in doing so. This incident happened years ago in a Southern church when a visiting brother approached the pastor at the time of the evening prayer

47

service and asked if he might have an opportunity to speak at the service. In doing so, he presented to the pastor a large folio made up of letters of commendation. But the pastor had the hunch that he should not give him a place on the program and declined to invite him to speak. The same visiting minister (if minister in truth he was) went to a neighboring church with the same petition and on Wednesday night was allowed to speak. The guest minister had hardly begun his message when a member of the church shouted, to the temporary dismay of all, "You are an imposter! I know who you are; I know your past! You dare not speak from this pulpit." In his words of reply, the guest minister closed his Bible and took his leave from the congregation at that moment.

Paul met his accusers bravely and openly, without fear of rebuke, saying:

> **You are our letter written in our hearts, known and read by all men; for you are becoming known as an epistle of Christ, cared for by us, written not with ink but with the Spirit of the Living God, not on tablets of stone but on heart tablets of flesh (vv. 2-3).**

There appears to be an allusion to this same thought in 1 Corinthians 9:2 when he said: "If to others I am not an Apostle, yet I am to you; for you are the seal of my apostleship in the Lord." These Christians in Corinth served to certify Paul's apostleship, and the letter that he had written in their hearts was authentic and was available for all to read. Notice how Paul refreshed the metaphor in saying that the Corinthians themselves were Christ's letters and that they were only in Paul's care and in the care of others like him who ministered to them. These letters were not written in black ink (made of soot, as a rule), but the pen that wrote them was dipped into the Spirit of the living God, for Paul's words here call to mind the prophecies of Jeremiah (31:33): "I will put my law in their inward hearts and in their hearts will I write it." (See also Ezek. 11:19; 36:26.)

(2) The Ministers of the New Covenant (vv. 4-6)

In verses 4 and 5 Paul stated unequivocally the ground of his confidence:

> For we have such self-confidence through Christ toward
> God. Not that we are qualified, of ourselves, to take credit for
> anything, as from ourselves, for our capability is from God
> (vv. 4-5).

Paul had no misgivings concerning his own qualifications. His
spiritual abilities were not something that came to him by nature.
They were not the fruit of natural development, and he wanted
the Corinthians to understand clearly his disposition to give God
credit for everything. He claimed no credit for anything for himself. Note that Paul used twice the same pronoun *(ek)* "as from
ourselves . . . *(ek)* from God." God is the source of whatever
capability Paul had and he desired no credit for it. After all, is it
not the Lord who gives to all of us whatever talents we have? All
of the spiritual gifts that are placed in the care of God's children
come from God, and Him alone. When Midori, the young Japa-
nese violin prodigy, was heard in a concert, one of the hearers
remarked, "That is genius." A friend close by remarked, "No!
That is a gift straight from God." How right are the words of the
latter for, when little Midori was only six years of age she gave an
astounding performance with her violin in Osaka, and the people
knew then that in this little wisp of a girl were talents seldom
given to a musical performer—maybe not more than one in every
fifty years.

Paul went on to acknowledge more fully the mission of Christians who had received talents from God:

> Who has qualified us (rendered us fit) to be servants of the
> new covenant, not of the letter but of the Spirit; for the letter
> kills but the Spirit gives life (v. 6).

Paul defined the intended character of ministers of the new
covenant: they are to be *servants,* "not of the letter but of the
Spirit." So one is confronted with the hard fact of the frightful
contrast between the religion of authority and the religion of the
Spirit. "The former leads to death; the latter, to life" (Herring, *in
loco*). The former has its moments of prestige and authority; but,
like the earthborn priests of the Old Testament, they passed away
and had to be followed by others who, as they, were likewise

mortal. Whatever glory or authority religious leaders have is like a vapor, a bit of mist in the form of a cloud in the air that is soon gone and passes away. But the glory of the Spirit is eternal and passes not away. Did Paul at the time of the writing of these words recall the prophecy of Jeremiah? Very likely he did.

Paul's argument is not intended to belittle the spiritual character of the law, but to say that the law itself, without the illuminating character and energizing force of the Spirit, cannot give life. Jesus stated unequivocally that He did not come to "destroy" the law or the prophets, but to fulfill their intended mission. All of the Old Testament, as the late Dr. John R. Sampey used to say, "slants upward." But it is only when the illuminating presence of Jesus Christ entered the scene in His incarnation, that the "letter" of the law received the needed illumination to enable one to interpret the real character and purpose of the law. All of this calls to mind the ancient blood sacrifices, in the order of the priesthood, which passed away. When Jesus Christ shed His blood on the cross and rose from the dead, He became the great High Priest whose ministry goes on forever. Not to be succeeded was He, as were the high priests of old, for they were mortal and died as other men. Greater then is the letter of the New Covenant because its glory is eternal whereas the glory of the old covenant was a passing thing and could only point to the coming of the New Covenant. And the New Covenant, under the cover of the Spirit, gives life whereas the letter "kills" (v. 6).

(3) The Ministry of Death and Life in Contrast (vv. 7-8).

Now if the ministry of death engraved in letters on stones came into existence in glory, so that the children of Israel could not look intently into the face of Moses on account of the glory of his face, glory that was passing away, how much more in glory will be the ministry of the Spirit?

Again, let us recall that Paul in no way intended to criticize the law and its mission in the Old Testament. Romans 7:12, for instance, called the law "holy" meaning righteous and whole and good. Paul was saying here that as good as the law was and as gracious as it was, it was still but a schoolmaster preparing the way for the coming of the New Covenant, a covenant of a righteousness that imparts life and a covenant that is engraved on the flesh of human hearts. The stark contrast is between legalism and spiritualism, a contrast that found expression in the Jewish mission and the Christian apostolate (3:7-11). Paul went on to say:

(4) Glory in the Ministry (vv. 9-11)

For if there was glory in the ministry of the condemnation, by much more does the ministry of righteousness abound in glory (v. 9).

In other words, the glory of the old covenant was "being done away," for in the New Covenant the high priest is Jesus and He is eternal. There would be no replacement as in the Old Covenant where one high priest would die and another would be appointed to follow in his train. The office and service of Moses issued in death, death to him and to all mortal men who followed him in service. Here again the contrast is clearly seen in that "by the works of the law shall no flesh be justified in His sight" (Rom. 3:20). For the righteousness of God, as realized in the New Covenant, is the righteousness manifested "now apart from the law" (Rom. 3:21).

For that which has been made glorious has not been made glorious, in this respect, on account of the surpassing glory (of the New Covenant) (v. 10).

Paul went on to point out the surpassing glory of the New Covenant, but this was not done merely to detract from the glory of the Old Testament. The two covenants were different. The glory that Moses received, and by which he was surrounded, remained limited in this respect. The glory of which Paul spoke brought out the contrast between the old and new. Moses was an apostle of the law; the ministry of the Spirit of the New Covenant, and of its righteousness was not entrusted to him. He could only pave the way for the coming of the eternal, the righteousness that God imparts, apart from the law which was, in itself in this respect, "the ministry of condemnation and of death" (Barrett).

For if that which passes away was through glory, by how much more that which remains is in glory (v. 11).

The restriction, the glory which was manifested in the ministry of the old covenant, is obvious in view of the freedom made possible by the New Covenant of love and salvation, not determined by human effort, but by God's gift. There is nothing "passing" about the gospel of the New Covenant, for it is here to stay. It is "God's last word indeed and cannot be superseded" (Barrett).

(5) Hardened Hearts and the Veil (vv. 12-16)

Having therefore a hope such as this, we act with great boldness in speech, and not as Moses did who put a veil upon his face so the children of Israel should not look intently into the conclusion of that which was passing away (vv. 12-13).

The meaning of Paul's words concerning the veil which Moses put over his face can best be taken as a sign that the old order was passing, the framework of the law in which the ministry of Moses and all the Old Testament leaders was rooted. In the New Covenant, persons would not be justified and find salvation by keeping the law; rather by the grace of God they would be saved by faith (Eph. 2:8-9). Again, let us note that this was not to discredit the law. The law had its place, and it served to the glory of God. But its service could not be compared with the religious framework of the New Covenant, which rests upon the gospel. It was into this new order that Paul became rooted following his Damascus experience. Even though the old order was temporal, in a state of abolition, it was veiled to the view of the children of Israel; otherwise it would have been a traumatic experience that could even have brought about the indictment of Moses as the leader of the passing scene. The imagery, of course, is difficult— Moses unwilling to share his insight at the moment with the children of Israel.

But their minds became hardened, and for this reason unto this day the same veil that in Christ is abolished remains unlifted in the public reading of the old covenant (v. 14).

The coming of Christ and His atoning act on the cross of Calvary brought an end to the bondage of the law as an instrument of salvation, but the children of Israel could not see this; they had a mental block which dulled their perception concerning the significance of the law as it relates to the coming Messiah. The institution of the new order took place in the ministry of Jesus, and until He is acknowledged as the Messiah, as the Savior who delivers man from sin, the veil remains.

> **Accordingly until this day when Moses is read, a veil lies upon their hearts. But whenever it shall turn to the Lord the veil is taken away (vv. 15-16).**

Christ alone can lift the veil so that His face can be seen and His purpose realized for the lost world; but this takes place only when the sinner turns to Him in faith and seeks forgiveness and reconciliation. Otherwise, the veil continues to lie upon the heart, whether of Israel or of humanity as a whole.

(6) Freedom (vv. 17-18)

> **Now the Lord is the Spirit; and where the Spirit of the Lord is, *there is* freedom (v. 17).**

The Holy Spirit, in the New Testament, is interchangeably called the Spirit of Christ and the Spirit of God (Rom. 8:9f.). It seems that what Paul was trying to explain has to do with the *freedom* that comes to the believer in the New Covenant, the perfect freedom of access to God without fear as in Exodus 34:34. No veil is necessary, for each believer is at liberty to commune directly with God. This concept of freedom is far removed from that of the old covenant. When a person is "in Christ" (2 Cor. 5:17) a marvelous change is brought about in which the person becomes a "new creation," "a new creature," where old things have passed away. The old life-style is gone forever. In this new relationship, the believer has freedom from the bondage of sin and freedom from the bondage of law. The death and resurrection of Christ assure the believer of his own resurrection at the last day. God truly writes His law in the human heart, with the pen of the Spirit, and the legalistic character of the old order then becomes a thing of the past. But the believer must understand that this newfound freedom is in no way to be thought of as a "license" to live one's life regardless of the commandments of God and the teachings of Jesus Christ in the New Testament. Some translators have tampered with verse 18, but the literal translation of the passage, it seems to me, makes the meaning clear enough. In itself it in no way serves to break down the concept of the Trinity.

> But we all with unveiled face keep on reflecting, as in a mirror, the glory of the Lord, being transformed into the same likeness, from glory unto glory, just as from the Spirit of the Lord (v. 18).

2 CORINTHIANS 4

¹Therefore having this ministry which we received as a gracious gift, we do not lose heart;

²rather having renounced the things hidden from a sense of shame, not going about in an underhanded way, or deceitfully using the word of God, we commend ourselves to every conscience of men in the sight of God.

³And even if our gospel is veiled, it is veiled in them who are perishing, ⁴in whom the god of this age has blinded their unbelieving minds so that they do not see the light of the gospel of the glory of Christ, who is the image of God.

⁵For we preach not ourselves, but Jesus Christ the Lord, and ourselves your slaves for Jesus' sake.

⁶For it is God who said, "Out of darkness a Light will shine," and who has shone in our hearts to bring to light the knowledge of the glory of God in the face of Christ.

⁷But we hold this treasure in earthen vessels that the surpassing greatness of the power may be of God and not from us.

⁸We are hard pressed in every way, but not crushed, disturbed, but not in despair.

⁹persecuted but not forsaken, cast down yet not destroyed.

¹⁰Always bearing about in the body the putting to death of Jesus so that the life of Jesus may also be manifested in our own bodies;

¹¹for we who are living are continually being handed over to death, for Jesus' sake, that the life of Jesus may also be manifested in our mortal bodies.

¹²For this reason death is at work in us, but life in you.

¹³Moreover, having the same spirit of faith, according to that which is written, I believed, therefore I spoke; and we believe also and for this reason we also speak,

¹⁴knowing that He who raised up the Lord Jesus will also raise us up together with Jesus and present us together with you (in God's presence).

¹⁵For all these things are for the sake of you, so that grace being multiplied through the multitude (of believers) may cause thanksgiving to abound unto the glory of God.

¹⁶For this reason we do not lose heart; and although our outward man be destroyed, yet our inward *man* is renewed day by day.

¹⁷For our present insignificant affliction produces in us an eternal weight of glory beyond all measure and proportion,

¹⁸while not keeping our eyes on the things that are seen, but on the things that are not seen; for things that are seen are transitory, but things that are not seen are eternal.

4

The Treasure and the Earthen Vessels

2 Corinthians 4:1-15

In the closing verses of chapter 3, Paul contrasted his own ministry with that of Moses. He made it clear, of course, that his apostleship was only representative and that the glory of the law was a fading, passing thing. The approach of ancient Israel to God was a fading glory, a glory that passed away in the face of the glory of the Lord manifested in the believer's relationship to God as he is actually transformed "into the same likeness, from glory unto glory, just as from the Spirit of the Lord" (v. 18).

Paul walked the tightwire, maintaining a perfect balance between his outward burdens as a minister of the gospel and the sublime glory of his internal existence and witness as a servant of Christ. If his words could be translated into music, we might well say that he ran the entire major scale, striking middle C with a thunderous pounding that was picked up by middle C in the hearts of his readers. How true this is today with the contemporary preachers of the Word. Every time the minister enters the pulpit and proclaims without fear or favor the glorious gospel of Christ, that proclamation will be picked up by sympathetic hearts throughout the audience. There will be some who are only half awake and who will wear a quizzical expression on their faces; for them the truth may explode, at a later hour, like a spiritual bomb in their hearts.

(1) Jesus Christ the True Light (vv. 1-6)

Therefore having this ministry which we received as a gracious gift, we do not lose heart; rather having renounced the things hidden from a sense of shame, not going about in an

underhanded way, or deceitfully using the word of God, we
commend ourselves to every conscience of men in the sight
of God (vv. 1-2).

In these few words Paul commended his own ministry not only
in the sight of mankind, but also in the sight of God. He made it
abundantly clear that his turnaround, his conversion and full acceptance of Jesus Christ as his Savior and Lord was complete
and final. He also wanted the Corinthians to know that, so far as
he was concerned, there was no such thing for the convinced
believer as losing heart. There was no deceit or craftiness to be
found in his handling of the Word of God. Everything he said
and did was subjected to the light of truth, and he asked for nothing more than for the conscience of persons to recognize and
accept that manifestation of the truth. After all, his ministry had
come to him as a gracious gift from God, and everything in his
ministry took place because of that gift of mercy. Paul's sincerity
was evident in every word he spoke. He did not adulterate the
gospel; he did not rely upon his own eloquence or his own brilliant understanding to gain acceptance. He merely held forth
God's shining Word. He was no joke teller trying to gain the attention of his audience. He caught the attention of the Corinthians with the direct appeal of the truth of the gospel itself.

**And even if our gospel is veiled, it is veiled in them who are
perishing, in whom the god of this age has blinded their unbelieving minds so that they do not see the light of the gospel
of the glory of Christ, who is the image of God (vv. 3-4).**

Paul uttered a telling word in these two verses, concerning the
response of people to the gospel of Christ. For some, the proclamation had little meaning, for in them the gospel was veiled. But
the veil, Paul said, was spread over their eyes by the "god of this
age" who blinded their eyes because they had unbelieving
minds. They simply did not see the "light of the gospel" though it
dealt with Christ, "who is the image of God." Apparently they did
not have an open mind, and that kind of person is difficult to deal
with. Any scientist who is perceptive keeps an open mind, for he
constantly searches for truth in the field of his mission. He is not

particularly interested, one would think, in the matter of who gets
the credit, as was true in the case of Dr. Jonas Salk, who wanted
to see the awful scourge of polio eradicated. Even so, the true
messenger of the gospel of Christ is ready and willing to be
merely a bystander so far as the credit for the transformation is
concerned. The selfish desire for personal credit for anything that
relates to the advancement of Christ's kingdom on earth must be
an abomination in the heart of God.

> For we preach not ourselves, but Jesus Christ the Lord, and
> ourselves your slaves for Jesus' sake. For it is God who said,
> "Out of darkness a Light will shine," and who has shone in
> our hearts to bring to light the knowledge of the glory of God
> in the face of Christ (vv. 5-6).

The thought in these two verses might be pondered well by
every Sunday School teacher, every lecturer on spiritual things,
and every minister of the gospel. Paul retired into the back-
ground, saying "we preach not ourselves, but Jesus Christ the
Lord." How wonderful it would be if all the servants of God
would embody these thoughts in mind and heart as they go out
to serve congregations, whether large or small in number! It is
here that Paul revealed both humility and meekness at its best;
and without these two shining qualities of commitment, no proclaimer of the Word can be at his best. But notice how Paul likewise declared that he was not only a servant of the Lord, but also
a servant of the Corinthians: "ourselves your slaves for Jesus'
sake." And this relationship, said Paul, was brought about *because of Jesus*. In verse 6, Paul came to the heart of the matter
declaring that it was all the fulfillment of the prophecy of God
who said "out of darkness a Light will shine." And the purpose of
that Light which had shone in the heart of Paul and the Corinthians was for a stated purpose, namely, "to bring to light the
knowledge of the glory of God in the face of Christ."

Maybe it is at this point that Christians fail miserably today. It is
easy for one to rejoice in one's own salvation and to regard it as a
sort of insurance policy so far as the future of the soul is concerned; but to react to that blessed experience in a viable way in
bringing to light this new knowledge of the glory of God so that it

may be shared by others, is an altogether different matter. It is not enough, for instance, for missionary societies merely to invest their time and talents in funding missionary endeavor engaged in by others. Every Christian, as a brother in Russia said to me, should be a missionary himself in helping to bring the light of the gospel to others. Paul's declaration concerning his own relationship to the gospel was in no sense to be regarded as a blandishment of his own spiritual efforts to make the gospel known to all people. Flattery itself must have been the remotest thought that could have come to his mind; for the most careful examination of his life and work hardly reveals a single iota of this mood.

(2) The Treasure and the Earthen Vessels (vv. 7-12)

But we hold this treasure in earthen vessels that the surpassing greatness of the power may be of God and not from us (v. 7).

The point here is that the receptacle of the gospel is earthen, and this accents the frailty of the vessel. Among the ancients, earthen vessels were sometimes looked upon as "symbols of weakness." And it could be that Paul used this symbolism to stress the human frailty of those who serve as receptacles for the gospel. The prophet Jeremiah (18:1-4) pointed out the resemblance between God as the potter and his chosen people as the potter's vessel. Paul wanted it to be clearly understood that the "surpassing greatness" of God's power comes from God, not from man. That concept in itself is enough to make for meekness and humility on the part of the human messenger of God. And this concept of the relationship between the human and the divine places the mission of the messenger in a category that is separate and unique. The message itself amounts to a "treasure" and is literally beyond compare. And the disregard of the character of this treasure has led to some of the most damaging religious scandals of the centuries—as the life-styles of a few TV evangelists reveal.

We are hard pressed in every way, but not crushed, disturbed, but not in despair, persecuted but not forsaken, cast down yet not destroyed (vv. 8-9).

We have here what Jean Herring has called "unique optimistic pessimism." That is how it needs to be with every true messenger of God. There will be times in the course of the pilgrimage when everything seems to cave in around the messenger with alarming portents. When such days come, the Christian is to remember that the messengers of Christ will always have their *ups and downs*. Such is to be expected. But there is the supportive love of divine providence to offer refuge and needed light for the way. For the true messenger of God, whatever the human situation, God offers a way out! Though the servant of God is momentarily at his wit's end and the plight is at its worst, he will not be "crushed" or destroyed. All the messenger needs to do is to lean upon the source of power and to kneel and look up to God with a heart of meekness and humility in waiting for God's merciful deliverance. Paul experienced the worst that could come to him at the hands of sinful men; but he got up from the devastating experience and went on with his mission.

> **Always bearing about in the body the putting to death of Jesus so that the life of Jesus may also be manifested in our own bodies; for we who are living are continually being handed over to death, for Jesus' sake, that the life of Jesus may also be manifested in our mortal bodies. For this reason death is at work in us, but life in you (vv. 10-12).**

Here the scene changes as Paul turned to the eschatological perspective. All of us who are servants of Christ share in His death just as we share in His cross. As to the cross, the cross of the Christian amounts to his own part in the cosmic effort of God to project through the ministry of Christ, the open door of salvation to the lost world. Here we have a picture of the old Adam and the new Adam. The old Adam had to die so that the new Adam could come into being, the transformation in which the old things have passed away and all things have become new. In the death of the old Adam, the physical life is preserved, but in the new Adam there takes place an actual manifestation of the risen life of Jesus in the mortal bodies of the believers. So, let the work of death go on; for the "life in you" goes on all the same, from stage unto stage of the glorious manifestation of the mighty power of God through Christ working in the life of mortal man. Actually this brings luster to the witness experiences in the life of a believer.

4. The Role of Faith (4:13 to 5:10)

> Moreover, having the same spirit of faith, according to that which is written, I believed, therefore I spoke; and we believe also and for this reason we also speak, knowing that He who raised up the Lord Jesus will also raise us up together with Jesus and present us together with you (in God's presence). For all these things are for the sake of you, so that grace being multiplied through the multitude (of believers) may cause thanksgiving to abound unto the glory of God (4:13-15).

Paul brought into focus the glorious aspect of the resurrection that is to be at God's appointed time in the future. Believers are to be raised up with Jesus, and the certainty of this truth becomes the keystone in the arch of Christian faith. Apart from Jesus' resurrection, every promise Jesus made would crumble into dust. He had to rise from the grave, and so do we, if there is to be any meaning to our faith. Paul professed his own faith in God, in Christ, and in the resurrection of the dead. And in doing so, he related his faith to the spoken word of the witness. "I believed," said Paul, "therefore I spoke." In other words, Paul's message concerning the gospel sprang out of the context of faith; for, apart from faith, there could be no viable message whether for Paul or for other believers. That is the way of the gospel. Notice also how all of this is tied in with knowledge. It is on the basis of experiential knowledge, "knowing that." Paul's message did not deal with doubts. And it is to be hoped that no preacher will ever deal with his doubts in the pulpit, but will devote his message to the proclamation of what he knows and believes about the gospel of Christ. Of course, for the messenger to proclaim the gospel of Christ effectively, he must be anointed by the Spirit. Still the messenger must at all times be undergirded with knowledge as well as with faith, for such is the proclamation of God's truth in Christ Jesus.

(1) The Seen and the Unseen (4:16-18)

For this reason we do not lose heart; and although our out-ward man be destroyed, yet our inward *man* is renewed day by day. For our present insignificant affliction produces in us an eternal weight of glory beyond all measure and propor-tion, while not keeping our eyes on the things that are seen, but on the things that are not seen; for things that are seen are transitory, but things which are not seen are eternal.

Paul declared that, in spite of his trials, he never lost heart, for he was conscious of the fact that, not withstanding the destruc-tion of the outward man, the inward man is renewed day by day. Paul did not seem to have in mind a doctrine of dualism here, for the old physical side of Adam and the new Adam go on side by side. The new man is the transformed man that rests in the same old body. Both the old Adam and the new Adam are here now with death coming to the physical side of Adam, while, day by day, spiritual renewal comes to the new Adam.

Paul gave us here added insight into the character of salvation. Though believers are *truly saved* (have salvation), spiritual re-newal continues to go on in the life of the believer in proportion to his faith and his lifelong effort to present himself as a living sacrifice to God to be used unto His glory. After all, present afflic-tions are "insignificant" when compared with the "eternal weight of glory" produced in the believer which is "beyond all measure and proportion." These insignificant tribulations are productive because God "works with us" in all things unto good for those that "love God" and are called "according to his purpose" (Rom. 8:28). And all of this emphasizes the fact that whatever trials and tribulations may come to the believer in the course of his witness to God's glory, he is to regard them as nothing more than trifles, affairs of circumstance which are trivial in significance. And the secret to this spiritual outlook, or wise understanding of things, rests in the ability of the messenger not to keep his eyes "on the things that are seen," "but on the things that are not seen"; for the things that are seen are transitory, but the things which are not seen are eternal.

Paul could hardly have stated his premise in a simpler manner. He made it clear that it is necessary for the Christian to fix his attention on the invisible aspects of his relationship with Christ and on the glory that rests in His resurrection from the dead. The believer is also to contemplate the manifestation of his own faith and works as he looks toward his own resurrection from the dead at the last day. This glorious hope has a sustaining power that is without measure. The physical body, the earthen vessel, is continually subjected to the process of death, while the spiritual self, the true self, continues to experience the daily renewal of God's divine grace. And undergirding all of this is the glad consciousness of the eventual consummation of this renewal at the last day.

[1]For we know that, if our earthly house of the physical body is destroyed, we have a building that comes from God, a house not made by human hands, eternal in the heavens.

[2]For verily in this estate we continue to sigh, longing to be clothed with our dwelling that is from heaven;

[3]so that, if we are clothed in this manner, we shall not be found naked.

[4]In truth, we who live in this physical body continue to groan, being burdened, because we do not wish to be unclothed, but to be clothed, that death may be swallowed up by life.

[5]Now He who created us for this very thing is God, who has given us the pledge of the Spirit.

[6]Being, therefore, always confident and knowing that while we are at home in the body, we are away from the Lord;

[7]for we walk about through faith, not through sight;

[8]and we are confident and also prefer, rather, to be absent from the body and to be at home with the Lord.

[9]For this reason we are ambitious to be well pleasing to Him whether we are at home or away.

[10]For we must all appear before the judgment seat of Christ, that each may receive a recompense for what he has done through his body, whether good or bad.

[11]Knowing therefore the fear of the Lord, we persuade men, but we are made manifest to God; and I hope also to be known in your conscience.

[12]We are not again commending ourselves to you, but giving you an occasion of glorying on our behalf, so that you may have an answer for those who glory in appearance, not in heart.

[13]For whether we are out of our senses, it is for God; whether we are of sound mind, it is for you.

[14]For the love of Christ impels us, having reached the decision that, since One died for all, therefore all have died;

[15]and that He died for all so that the living should no longer live for themselves, but for Him who for their sake died and rose again for them.

[16]Consequently, from now on we know no man according to the flesh; even though we have known Christ according to the flesh, now we no longer know Him.

[17]Therefore if any person is in Christ, he is a new creature; the old things have passed away; behold, they have become new.

[18]But all things are from God, who reconciled us to Himself through Christ and gave unto us the ministry of reconciliation;

[19]so that as God was in Christ reconciling the world to Himself, not reckoning to them their trespasses, He has also committed to us the proclamation of the reconciliation.

[20]We are therefore ambassadors in behalf of Christ, as though God were entreating through us; we beseech you in behalf of Christ, be reconciled to God.

[21]Him who knew no sin He made to become sin in our behalf, so that we might become God's righteousness in Him.

5

The Role of Faith

2 Corinthians 4:13 to 5:10 (cont.)

Paul continued his discussion of the role of faith, begun in the preceding chapter (4:16) and in doing so he used an old word that emphasizes a state of acquired knowledge and perceptive understanding. He might have used another word *(ginōskō)* which conveys more of the idea *to come to know,* and which emphasizes the experiential side of the knowledge. Here the emphasis is on the downright sense of knowledge.

(2) The Earthly House (2 Cor. 5:1-5)

For we know that, if our earthly house of the physical body is destroyed, we have a building that comes from God, a house not made by human hands, eternal in the heavens. For verily in this estate we continue to sigh, longing to be clothed with our dwelling that is from heaven; so that, if we are clothed in this manner, we shall not be found naked (vv. 1-3).

Did Paul have in mind the ominous portent of his impending death, or his inability to complete his mission before his parting day? Whether his thoughts ran this way or not, one thing is clear in all of his words: the alternative is to be reunited with the Lord, and in that glad consciousness he had no doubt. In fact, his words in verse 2 expressed an actual longing to be with the Lord in the heavenly dwelling. Already he had said, "For to me to live is Christ, and to die is gain" (Phil. 1:21).

The figure here recalls the nomadic experiences of the dwellers in the Middle East in Paul's day. They lived in tents, tents made by human hands, put up by human hands and taken down by human hands. The figure was therefore an ever-changing one. The family would move from location to location for better grazing conditions for the cattle, better access to water, or more effective cultivation of crops; in each instance the tent was taken down and moved. Even so with the believer, if the house of the fleshly body be taken down and destroyed, another dwelling place awaits the believer, the house in the heavens that is "eternal." (In the apocalyptic literature there were references to the dwelling places of the faithful in times to come.) But this future place of dwelling of which Paul spoke, was an eternal thing, for it is a home established forever in the heavens. The physical body inhabits "an earthly tent"—the body is the tent. When it is of no more use, God has made provision for the future home of the believer. There is nothing insecure about this new dwelling place, nothing impermanent, as was true of the setting up and taking down of tents in the Middle East by the nomads.

What is the occasion of the "sigh" to which Paul referred? He was doubtless thinking about his many experiences of affliction, of trials, and tribulations. The figure of being "clothed with our [new] dwelling" constitutes a mixed metaphor. One puts on clothing, and wears it—but not so of a building. But the sense of what Paul said is clear. It might be well for the reader to turn to 1 Corinthians 15:53-55 and consider Paul's words there in the light of these words. Certainly one thing is evident: whether Paul thought of his death in terms of the return of our Lord, or whether he thought that, prior to that, there was a glorious body to be put on over the earthly body one day. And certainly one finds no conflict or "doctrinal contradiction" in the passage of 1 Corinthians 15:5.

> In truth, we who live in this physical body continue to groan, being burdened, because we do not wish to be unclothed, but to be clothed, that death may be swallowed up by life. Now He who created us for this very thing is God, who has given us the pledge of the Spirit (vv. 4-5).

Notice Paul's words (v. 4) "continue to groan" and "being burdened." The "sigh" or "groan" is a continuing thing. Certainly life for the apostle Paul was made up of one trial after another. His sufferings were innumerable in character and in intensity. Death really held no fear for Paul. He knew, on the basis of the promises of God, he would have as his inheritance "a building that comes from God." It would not be temporary as buildings made by human hands.

(3) The Pledge of the Spirit (vv. 6-10)

Paul's confidence rested on the fact that God created us all, by faith, for this "very thing" and gave us "the pledge of the Spirit" (v. 5). Paul made much of this pledge in the Ephesian letter in his discussion of the guaranteed relationship of believers: ". . . we who had put our hope beforehand in Christ; in whom you also, having heard the word of the truth, the gospel of your salvation, in whom also having believed (trusted) you were sealed with the Holy Spirit of the promise, who is a pledge (surety) of our inheritance unto the ransoming of his (God's) possession unto the praise of his glory" (Eph. 1:12-14). Here the word translated "pledge" is an old Greek word *arrabōn* which stood for a part of the purchase price of anything paid in advance which served as a guarantee and surety that the rest of the price in due time would be paid (A. T. Robertson). The Holy Spirit therefore was the down payment, God's gift, and the first part of the payment in Christ.

> Being, therefore, always confident and knowing that while we are at home in the body, we are away from the Lord; for we walk about through faith, not through sight; and we are confident and also prefer, rather, to be absent from the body and to be at home with the Lord. For this reason we are ambitious to be well pleasing to Him whether we are at home or away. For we must all appear before the judgment seat of Christ, that each may receive a recompense for what he has done through his body, whether good or bad (vv. 6-10).

Paul now rested his case on the highest possible spiritual plane. Incidental matters no longer disturbed him, even that of "nakedness" with regard to being "clothed" or "unclothed" on the final day. To be "at home in the body" simply means to be "away

from the Lord" (v. 6). After all, this earthly pilgrimage is a faith
matter; we walk through "faith" not through "sight"; and when
one clearly perceives this glorious truth, it is possible to come to
the place where one actually prefers rather "to be absent from the
body and to be at home with the Lord" (v. 8). Paul's affirmation is
not unlike that which he made in 1 Corinthians 13:12. Similar
assurance may also be found in his words in Romans 8:24ff. The
dilemma of life and death therefore had no problem for the apostle. His basic desire was to be near the Lord and to effectively
achieve the Lord's life-style and the realization of the divine purpose for which he had been called by the Lord when he was set
apart as a minister to the Gentiles at the time of the Damascus
experience. Not to be overlooked are Paul's words in verse 9
which clearly reflect the soul of his ambition, as far as his earthly
life-style is concerned: "to be well pleasing to Him whether we
are at home or away."

(4) The Central Fact (v. 10)

In verse 10 Paul brought the Corinthian Christians face to face
with the central fact of reality, namely, that there is a final judgment in which there will be for each one a "recompense" for what
he has "done through his body," whether good or bad. There is
much left unsaid in this passage that the believer would like to
know. But the naked fact is clear, that there is to be a judgment
day and some kind of grading with reference to the life-styles on
earth, and the decision will be based on the elements of that life
in the body, "whether good or bad."

The point does not have to do with the fact of whether the
person is saved or lost; it has to do rather with the manner in
which he has lived up to his opportunities and the commands of
Christ in view of his Christian commitment. Some will be saved,
as Paul pointed out in 1 Corinthians 3:15, "as by fire." In other
words, according to Paul's premise, every believer will be judged
according to his works and that is a fearful thing to contemplate.
He does not deal with the timing of the judgment, whether at
death or at the second coming. Surely the contemporary follower

of Christ needs to understand clearly that there is far more to the Christian confession than the mere acknowledgment before the public that Jesus Christ is Savior and Lord. There is a life to live, a life of obedience to God's commands, and the character of that life becomes the hallmark to the significance of his witness.

The matter of "good or bad" is not dealt with in detail. Paul does not deal in *gray* areas. Whatever the good or the evil is, the character of the deed is judged in its relationship to the commands of God and the realization of His holy purposes for the individual. Certainly the evil of which Paul spoke does not necessarily mean the breaking of one of the Ten Commandments. The deed, on the other hand, may be something paltry, something worthless, insignificant, insultingly small, but contemptible in the light of God's intent for the believer. It is at this point that many contemporary Christians need to pause to think of their day's activities and what they have done in the way of witness, both by word and deed, that will be of lasting good in the kingdom of our Lord.

5. The Ministry of Reconciliation (5:11 to 6:11)

Beginning with verse 11 the dialogue shifts to a more personal portrayal of Paul's own role in the ministry of reconciliation, as well as the role of all true believers. Certainly these verses reflect how the author felt about his own purpose as an apostle and his relationship to the apostolate in general. He reiterates his "sincerity of purpose."

(1) The Fear of the Lord (vv. 11-13)

Knowing therefore the fear of the Lord, we persuade men, but we are made manifest to God; and I hope also to be known in your conscience. We are not again commending ourselves to you, but giving you an occasion of glorying on our behalf, so that you may have an answer for those who glory in appearance, not in heart. For whether we are out of our senses, it is for God; whether we are of sound mind, it is for you.

The words "fear of the Lord" are not heard too often in the language of contemporary Christians; but the apostle Paul used the words without apology. He was always conscious of that fear, and out of that frame of reference came forth his effort to persuade people everywhere to turn to the Lord. Paul was not boasting. He knew that he, and every person, must stand before the judgment seat of Christ. He knew also that even here on the pilgrimage all are "made manifest to God." He also expressed the hope that the Corinthians themselves would be fully aware of the kind of person he was. He had nothing to hide. There were no sordid spots in his ministry to be sorted out and flaunted before the eyes of believers. He wanted to be known for the kind of person he was and the kind of person he hoped to become in Christ Jesus. Just as Paul *stood open* to God, Paul wanted also to stand open to the Corinthian congregation. While Paul in no sense was endeavoring to commend himself again to the Corinthian church, he did want to give the Corinthians an opportunity to glory in his behalf so that they might in turn have an answer to those "who glory in appearance, not in the heart" (v. 12). The adversaries abounded on every side, and they were known to the Corinthians. They were people who put a premium on appearances and whose glorying was not of the heart. They could not bring the real desires and the purposes of their souls to light. These were false apostles and were referred to by Paul in 4:1-2; 10:12; and 11:4,12-14,20. Paul's words "whether we are out of our senses" may have referred to speaking in tongues (1 Cor. 14) or visions (2 Cor. 12:1-7). But he wanted one thing clear about it: it was for God. Of course, Paul made known his views on the matter of tongues in his first letter to the Corinthians. He told them that he would rather speak five words that edify than ten thousand in a tongue. His purpose in whatever he did was to glorify the Lord, not man. Evidently many caustic reproaches had been hurled at the apostle. Some probably looked upon him as being mad, or out of his senses. But however they wanted to regard him, Paul assured them that his state of ecstasy was "for God."

(2) The Love of Christ (vv. 14-16)

**For the love of Christ impels us, having reached the decision
that, since One died for all, therefore all have died; and that
He died for all so that the living should no longer live for
themselves, but for Him who for their sake died and rose
again for them (vv. 14-15).**

Paul's words "the love of Christ impels us" basically mean
keeps us together, sustains us, and *urges us.* The passage could
be translated "Christ's love for us" or "our love for Christ," but I
regard the words "of Christ" to be subjective genitive, meaning
the love of Christ for Paul (v. 15). This love was so meaningful to
Paul that nothing could happen in his pathway that would divert
him from his mission to the Corinthians and to the world. Paul's
words "One died for all" referred to the historical fact of Christ's
death on the cross; and his words "therefore all have died" seem
to refer to the symbolic likeness of the death of the Christian,
seen in the death of his old manner of living, as he becomes the
new person in Christ. Everything about the old life-style that was
contrary to the mind and the will of Christ passed away.

This same fact is symbolized by the act of immersion in Christian baptism. Even as Christ died and was buried and raised from
the dead, so is it of the believer who identifies himself completely
with Christ by faith. Does the believer really die? Do those who
come to know Christ as Savior truly die? Of course not, physically. They still have their old physical bodies; however, the
bodies have been transformed in the mind and heart so that all
things are new. But the new life is lived *in Christ;* not for self, not
for gain, but "for Him who for their sake died and rose again for
them" (v. 15). It is all that simple. And so it was in the life of the
apostle Paul. And this was the reason for the death of Christ: He
died for all to the end that all should live for Him and for His
increasing kingdom on earth.

> **Consequently, from now on we know no man according to
> the flesh; even though we have known Christ according to
> the flesh, now we no longer know Him (v. 16).**

As a consequence of this new, divine relationship, the new birth, bound up with the dying of Christ and, symbolically with their own death, there emerges a divine consequence, namely, said Paul, "from now on we know no man according to the flesh" (v. 16). What did he mean by this? For one thing, the thoughts of the regenerate person differ from the thoughts of the unregenerate. He has a new kind of knowledge. He does not reckon in terms of the flesh. He does not look at and evaluate people in terms of the physical. In other words, the life of the regenerate person is no longer determined by the flesh; his existence is not purely corporal. He still has the gaze of the inner eye, but it is not focused on the carnal, on the earthly, on things limited to the world. The knowledge that Paul had in mind here is evidently knowledge that relates to things of the Spirit and that are produced by the spiritual influences of life. In this new order, the evaluation of human beings is not "according to the flesh." Just as the death and resurrection of Christ broke in upon the minds of believers an altogether new concept of truth, even so the believer no longer regards Him "according to the flesh." He is no longer looked upon in this manner. By His mighty act that brought redemption to all people, He is now looked upon as Savior, Redeemer, and Cleanser from sin.

(3) The New Creation (vv. 17-21)

Therefore if any person is in Christ, he is a new creature; the old things have passed away; behold, they have become new. But all things are from God, who reconciled us to Himself through Christ and gave unto us the ministry of reconciliation; so that as God was in Christ reconciling the world to Himself, not reckoning to them their trespasses, He has also committed to us the proclamation of the reconciliation (vv. 17-19).

Before the believer came to be reconciled through the redemptive love of Christ he was under the power of Satan, and lived in the realm of Satan's works. But when he came under the dominion of Christ's redeeming love, he was rescued, torn away from the powers of Satan and given deliverance for all time. By this mighty act of God on the part of every person who turns to Him with a repentant heart by faith, that person's debt is canceled. The redeemed one becomes justified and the glorious pilgrimage begun by which the one redeemed becomes a witness to the saving power of God in Christ. Paul made it clear that God is the reconciler and that Christ His Son is His intermediate Agent by which God affects the reconciliation and through which the ministry of reconciliation passes to the newly born followers of Christ. In verse 19 Paul stressed the role of the apostle in the redemptive process as it relates to contemporary Christians. Just as God was in Christ "reconciling the world to Himself, not reckoning to them their trespasses" (v. 19), even so He has drawn the redeemed ones into the reconciliation process and committed to them the mission of proclamation concerning that reconciliation. At bottom this means that all those who have become new persons in Christ are brought into the mission.

> We are therefore ambassadors in behalf of Christ, as though God were entreating through us; we beseech you in behalf of Christ, be reconciled to God. Him who knew no sin he made to become sin in our behalf, so that we might become God's righteousness in him (vv. 20-21).

In becoming ambassadors of Christ the believers share in the reconciliation effort and the message of the ambassador is stated clearly in verse 20: "We beseech you in behalf of Christ, be reconciled to God." The proclamation of ambassadors in behalf of Christ boils down to the point at which God, as it were, entreats through them. God needs no reconciliation. It is man, and man alone, who needs to be reconciled to God. To achieve this joyful relationship, the Savior and the saved share together in the mutual purpose of Christ who was "made to become sin in our behalf." Christ became identified with sin through His death on the cross, a mysterious identification with sin that recalls Deuteronomy 21:23 which declared "cursed is every one that hangeth on a tree." Christ took upon Himself the burden of the sins of all mankind. And in His sacrifice on the cross he became the eternal lamb of God, an eternal lasting sacrifice that delivers from the dominion of Satan all who come to Him by faith. Paul summed up the purpose and meaning of Christ's identification with sin through His death on the cross in saying that it took place "so that we might become God's righteousness in him" (v. 21).

2 CORINTHIANS 6

¹And as we work together *with Him,* we also appeal to you not to receive the grace of God in vain;

²for He says, "At a favorable time, I listened to you, and in a day of deliverance, I came to your aid." See, now is the welcome time; behold, now is the day of salvation,

³giving no one an occasion for stumbling in any way, that the ministry be not blamed;

⁴but in everything, presenting ourselves as ministers of God with much patience: in tribulations, in distresses, in difficulties,

⁵in wounds, in imprisonments, in disturbances, in sleeplessness, in labors, in fastings,

⁶in purity, in knowledge, in self-control, in kindness, in the Holy Spirit, in love without hypocrisy,

⁷in the word of truth, in the power of God, through the armor of righteousness, on the right hand and on the left,

⁸through glory and dishonor, through evil report and good report, through being taken as imposters, *while yet* true men,

⁹as unknown and yet well known, as dying and yet alive, as undergoing punishment and yet not put to death,

¹⁰as being sorrowful yet always rejoicing, as being poor yet making many rich, as having nothing yet possessing everything.

¹¹Our mouth has spoken freely to you, O Corinthians, our heart is open wide (to you);

¹²you are not subjected by us, but you are restricted by your own hearts.

¹³Now for a similar recompense, (I speak to you as to children) you must also open wide your hearts too.

¹⁴Do not become mismated with unbelievers; for what companionship can there be between righteousness and lawlessness, or what close relationship in light and darkness?

¹⁵And what harmony is there of Christ with Belial, or what has the believer in common with the disbeliever?

¹⁶And what agreement is there between the temple of God and idols? For we ourselves are the temple of the living God; just as God said, "I will dwell in them, and walk about among them, and I will be their God, and they will be my people."

¹⁷"Therefore, come out from their midst and be separate," says the Lord, "and touch not what is unclean, and I will receive you";

¹⁸and I will be a father to you, and you will be to me sons and daughters," says the Lord Almighty.

6

The Ministry of Reconciliation

2 Corinthians 5:11 to 6:11 (cont.)

In the preceding chapter Paul said, "We are therefore ambassadors in behalf of Christ, as though God were entreating through us" (2 Cor. 5:20). In continuing his discussion of the ministry of reconciliation, he introduced the idea of collaboration on the part of the ambassador of Christ, with God, who is the source of the authority of the messenger as a proclaimer of God's mission in Christ.

(4) God's Fellow Workers (2 Cor. 6:1)

And as we work together *with Him*, we also appeal to you not to receive the grace of God in vain.

Some of the translators, notably Chrysostom, took this passage to indicate Paul's collaboration with the Corinthians. Of course, the matter of witnessing to the gospel of Christ is a cooperative endeavor, in a way, with all witnesses. For while we are fellow workers with God in Christ, we are also fellow workers one with another. It seems better however in the light of 5:20, and in the light of the verses that follow, to think of this particular phase of the collaboration as being with God. After all, Paul regarded himself as being God's ambassador. And so, all of us who profess to be Christ's followers are God's co-workers, God's partners (1 Cor. 3:9). The main point in this passage however is Paul's appeal for a worthy response on the part of those who receive the grace of God. His plea is that it not be received "in vain" (v. 1). This points up the problem that plagues the churches throughout the world today, the problem brought about by the failure on the part of the acknowledged followers of Christ who "receive the grace of God in vain." What did Paul mean by the words "in vain"? The warning appears to be directed at the failure of Christians to bear fruit. Christianity, by divine intent, is a fruit-bearing religion. The gospel message is related to every facet of human endeavor and human interrelationships. There is no such thing as a purely social gospel. The gospel of Christ is related to every facet of society, and fruit bearing is to take place in every area of the interchange of human relations. From Paul's words in 1 Corinthians it is obvious that there were those among the Corinthians who were failing to bear fruit. If the recipient of the grace of God does not react worthily, in return for the grace so fruitfully given, he nullifies the character of the grace as it relates to him.

(5) The Day of Salvation (v. 2)

For He says, "At a favorable time, I listened to you, and in a day of deliverance, I came to your aid." See, now is the welcome time; behold, now is the day of salvation.

Paul in no sense intended to imply here that the present is the only "welcome time," the only day of salvation. There is no time limit as to the day of salvation other than the limit the unbeliever places upon the matter by his own response. But there is a passing of religious opportunity. One may constantly say no to God, turn one's back upon the promises of God and resist the pleadings of the Spirit if one wishes to do so; but by so much one will come to have an ear that is hard of hearing and a heart that is irresponsible to God's entreaties. Christ, by His atoning sacrifice and His resurrection from the dead, made every day, through all the ages, a welcome time for the reception of the gospel. The gospel is for everyone of every race and nation, and the path that leads to the reception of salvation is the pathway of grace through faith. (Eph. 2:8-9) See Isaiah 49:8 for the source of Paul's quotation.

(6) Safeguarding the Ministry of Reconciliation (vv. 3-10)

Giving no one an occasion for stumbling in any way, that the ministry be not blamed; but in everything, presenting

ourselves as ministers of God with much patience: in tribulations, in distresses, in difficulties, in wounds, in imprisonments, in disturbances, in sleeplessness, in labors, in fastings, in purity, in knowledge, in self-control, in kindness, in
the Holy Spirit, in love without hypocrisy, in the word of
truth, in the power of God, through the armor of righteousness, on the right hand and on the left, through glory and
dishonor, through evil report and good report, through being
taken as imposters, *while yet* true men, as unknown and yet
well known, as dying and yet alive, as undergoing punishment and yet not put to death, as being sorrowful yet always
rejoicing, as being poor yet making many rich, as having
nothing yet possessing everything.

Paul had experienced in his own life irritating faultfinding on
the part of critics. He knew the feel of vitriolic censure by his
enemies. He also wanted the Corinthians to jealously guard
themselves against any word or deed that might lead to censure
and faultfinding concerning the ministry. It is not difficult to see
the relevance of Paul's words here in the light of the contemporary experiences of believers. The damage done to the bearers of
the gospel in general by such wild, immoral escapades can
hardly be measured. Paul did not hesitate to position himself in
such matters by saying, "If meat causes my brother to stumble, I
will eat no more while the world stands" (1 Cor. 8:13).

Here Paul literally ran the gamut of representative acts of
wrongdoing that could vitiate the character of the ministry. He
wanted the Corinthians to guard against any and all words or
deeds that might impair the quality of the ministry or make it in
any way faulty in the eyes of unbelievers. He wanted nothing
done that would corrupt, debase, or pervert the shining quality of
the labors of the true ministers of God. Paul in these brilliant,
fearless, articulate words of warning laid bare his very soul.

There is little need here to break down and classify these erratic vagaries of human perversion that could, and at times do,
cause censure to be heaped upon the heads of those who serve
worthily. One bad apple can easily become a spoiler for those
around it.

One might raise a worthy question at this point: is it possible for a bearer of the good tidings so to desert God's intended behavior for him in the pursuit of his mission as to disqualify himself for the role of the minister in future days? Certainly the matter of forgiveness is not the issue here. It is the matter of an irresponsible life-style on the part of those who should be truly regarded as worthy of emulation.

Paul spoke out of his own bitter experience. As a minister of the gospel, he had been in "tribulations, in distresses, in difficulties, in wounds, in imprisonments, in disturbances, in sleeplessness, in labors, in fastings." And in these bitter moments of conflict he had proved himself to be a worthy minister of God *with much patience.*

Every young minister facing his God-called task should find a quiet place for meditation and consider these arresting words of admonition that came from a veteran minister who has been through the fires of fearful encounters with those who would destroy him.

Whether or not Paul intended for it to be so, these verses of admonition, out of his own personal experience, form a commentary on his own life and works. Paul knew the meaning of the words "glory" and "disgrace." He knew the meaning of full acceptance on the part of believers and, on the other hand, the depressing effects of rejection. Still nothing that happened to him deterred him. Unrecognized by men as an apostle, yet he was recognized by God and considered himself to be not one step behind the super-apostles.

Notice how paradoxical Paul's words became. "As dying and yet alive, as undergoing punishment and yet not put to death" (v. 9).

As Paul continued to speak of the vicissitudes of life, note the antitheses (v. 8): "through glory and dishonor, through evil report and good report, through being taken as imposters, while yet true men." For Paul's fuller discussion of the armor of God and the weapons of righteousness, turn to Ephesians 6:11ff., and to Romans 6:13.

In spite of the caustic and all but overwhelming experiences of

life, Paul was able to continue to rejoice: "as being sorrowful yet
always rejoicing." He made it clear that there is no such thing as
poverty in the life that is truly spiritual. For though one may be
poor in regard to material things, the messenger of God is able to
make "many rich"; and while he possesses literally nothing in the
way of material things, he possesses everything in the realm of
the spirit (v. 10).

All through these words of admonition, Paul distinguished between the seen and the unseen, the reality and mere appearance. And in this perceptive understanding Paul could say in his
Letter to the Philippians: "I have strength for all things in Him
who endues me with power" (4:13). He could also say, "I have
learned in whatever circumstances I am to be content" (v. 11).
Indeed, at no other place in the Bible does one find such noble
praise, such a lofty portrayal of God's intended life-style for His
apostles on their divine mission.

(7) Freedom of Proclamation (vv. 11-13)

**Our mouth has spoken freely to you, O Corinthians, our
heart is open wide (to you); you are not subjected by us, but
you are restricted by your own hearts.**

Paul meant that he had kept nothing back "in his portrayal of
the glory of the ministry" (Robertson). He did not want the Corinthians to feel that there were any restrictions on his part, in his
words to the Corinthians, and likewise there would be no restrictions in his own heart concerning their freedom. Whatever restriction there might be was due to their point of view in their own
hearts.

When a young minister met with the leadership of a large
church to which he was soon to go as pastor, he asked this question near the midnight hour: "One thing I would like to know.
Will I have freedom in the pulpit of this church to speak as I
believe God directs me?" Paul felt that he had that freedom, and
he wanted the Corinthians to have the same feeling about him.
He wanted them to know that his heart was open to them. In his
comment on Paul at this point C. K. Barrett stated it well: "My

heart is wide open to you. There are no secrets in it: there is room for you in it, and I long to have you there." No matter what the adversaries of Paul may have said, the fact was he was not attempting to cramp, confine, or restrict them. The roots of any feeling they might have had concerning such were to be found in their own hearts.

One can only speculate on the words of Paul's adversaries that called forth his reply in verses 11-13. Did they accuse him of being a narrow-minded man in his sympathies? Did they try to convince others that in his cosmic outlook he would leave no room in his heart for the Corinthians? Whatever it was his adversaries said, Paul tried desperately to put a stop to it; and he spoke candidly in doing so, for he addressed them personally, "O Corinthians" (v. 11). The word translated "hearts" in verse 12 is an old word *(splagchnois)* that literally means *inward parts, entrails,* and is used figuratively *of the seat of the emotions.* It is also used to express *love, affection, sympathy;* but here the reference seems to be *the heart* in contrast to the word "heart" *(kardia)* in verse 11. In other words, if the Corinthians had genuine affection for Paul, they were to show it by opening wide their hearts to him. There really needs to be more of this kind of expression manifested between the pastor and the people in the contempo rary church. There should be nothing that is maudlin, of course, nothing that is tearfully, weakly, or foolishly sentimental, for genuine affection marked by the open heart needs to be felt by the pastor and the people—the street is two-way! Paul felt there was need of reciprocity. And this principle certainly should prevail between the pastor and his congregation.

> **Now for a similar recompense, (I speak to you as to children) you must also open wide your hearts too (v. 13).**

The word translated "recompense" carries the idea of something *in exchange,* as a *recompense in return for something.* In other words, Paul had opened wide his heart to the Corinthians, and he expected them to reciprocate by opening their hearts wide to him. His words "I speak to you as to children" represent an analogy which some regard to mean that the Corinthians should respond to him in respect and imitation, in things worthy, just as children do in their response to their parents.

6. The Call to the Separate Life (2 Cor. 6:14 to 7:1)

(1) Mismated Marriages

Do not become mismated with unbelievers; for what companionship can there be between righteousness and lawlessness, or what close relationship in light and darkness? (v. 14).

This passage which recalls Leviticus 19:19 and Deuteronomy 22:10, expressly forbids the believer to marry an unbeliever thereby producing a mixed marriage. Paul does not elaborate on the injunction; he simply leaves it there and his words are plain to the understanding. Proof is certainly not lacking in contemporary society concerning appropriateness of this command. If a lover, for instance, cannot succeed in witnessing effectively to an unbeliever with whom marriage is about to take place, the believer is to understand that the opportunity to win the mate to acceptance of Jesus Christ as Savior and Lord is far more likely to be achieved before marriage than after marriage.

In the old English are to be found the words "a good purchase," an expression that I heard an old, unlettered man use when he was trying to help lift a log from the ground onto the wagon. "Just wait a minute," he said, "until I get a good purchase," meaning that he wanted to get his feet planted firmly on the ground so he would not slide down the slanting ground while helping to lift the load. It is before marriage that the "better purchase" may be found for witnessing to the prospective mate.

In Deuteronomy 22:10 there is a reference of a different nature to the matter of being yoked together: "Thou shalt not plow with an ox and an ass together." But here (v. 14, KJV) Paul is saying literally "stop becoming unequally yoked with unconverted heathen." From his words, it is obvious that this sort of thing had been going on. The verb Paul used is the present imperative, which indicates clearly that such had been practiced among the Corinthians. But the implication of Paul's words is far wider than that of marriage alone. When a believer and an unbeliever get under the yoke together in a business undertaking, there are naturally two standards of values, two bases of evaluation. Will this not likely create problems when a moral point is at issue? Paul did not mince words in his direct thrust to the problem that must have existed among the Corinthians, and the Corinthians could hardly have misconstrued the meaning of his words. So as far as Paul was concerned, there was no place for a gray line between light and darkness, and between the believer and the unbeliever there could be no chameleon-like response on the part of the believer. This position needs to be crystal clear at all times where points of Christian morality are concerned.

> **And what harmony is there of Christ with Belial, or what has the believer in common with the disbeliever? (v. 15).**

Paul continued to enforce the antithesis of right and wrong. Although the opposition between the two is evident and the contrast marked, he continued to emphasize it. The line of demarcation between the believer and the unbeliever must be clear and uncompromising in all matters of faith and basic doctrines. If right is right, it is right forever. If wrong is wrong, it is wrong forever— that is, in matters of a moral nature when considered in the light of our Judeo-Christian concepts of truth and duty.

(2) The Temple of God (6:16 to 7:1)

> **And what agreement is there between the temple of God and idols? For we ourselves are the temple of the living God; just as God said, "I will dwell in them, and walk about among them, and I will be their God, and they will be my people" (v. 16).**

In verse 16 the contrast continues with the reference here to the "temple of God and idols." As if to butress his premise, the apostle went on to declare that the Christian is the "temple of the living God"; and, as if to prove that declaration, Paul called on God to witness concerning His dwelling place and His intimate fellowship with His people: "I will dwell in them, and walk about among them, and I will be their God, and they will be my peo-

ple." See Isaiah 52:11 and Ezekiel 20:33-34. The first part of
verse 16, of course, recalls 1 Corinthians 3:16 and 6:19, where
the people of God are identified as the temple of God. The verse
also recalls Ezekiel 37:27 and Leviticus 26:12.

In verse 17 Paul zeroed in on the problem with another sharp
command:

> **"Therefore, come out from their midst and be separate," says
> the Lord, "and touch not what is unclean, and I will receive
> you."**

The ringing call to the separate life is clear and unmistakable.
While the appeal does not call on the Christian to withdraw from
society as a whole, it does call for a great separation—the separation of the life-style of the believer as against the life-style of the
unbeliever. Notice that Paul identified with the Lord in his commandments ("says the Lord"). Paul had the authority to speak
such words on his own, but the latter part of the verse required
him to speak as he did. After all, it is the Lord who does the
receiving, and it is the Lord who laid down the guidelines for the
union of the believer with Christ.

> **"And I will be a father to you, and you will be to me sons and
> daughters," says the Lord Almighty (v. 18).**

These words that frequently occur in the Old Testament have
one additional thought that can be appropriately mentioned,
namely, the word "daughters." Daughters are of God just as the
sons are of God. Did Paul add the word "daughters" of God to
stress in a further way the equality of the sexes in the eyes of
God? Maybe so, for that is the way that it is. In Christ there is
neither male nor female.

2 CORINTHIANS 7

[1]Now that we have these promises, dear friends, let us cleanse ourselves from all defilement of body and spirit, perfecting our holiness in the fear of the Lord.

[2]Make room for us (in your hearts); we treated no one unjustly, we corrupted no one, we took advantage of no one.

[3]I say this not to condemn, for I told you before that you are in our hearts to die together and to live together.

[4]Great is my boldness in speech toward you; great is my pride in you. I am filled with encouragement; I am overflowing with joy in all our affliction.

[5]For even when we arrived in Macedonia our body had no relief; rather we were afflicted on every side—strife without, fears within.

[6]But God, who comforts the lowly, comforted us in the coming of Titus,

[7]and not only by his presence but also with the encouragement with which he was encouraged by you, as he reported to me your longing for me, your mourning, your warmth of feeling for me, so that I rejoiced still more.

[8]For even if I offended you in the latter, I do not regret it; even if I did regret it (for I now see that the letter irritated you for only a short time),

[9]now I rejoice, not that you were humiliated, but that you became sorrowful enough to repent; for you became sorrowful as God would have it, in order that you might in no way suffer injury by us.

[10]For the godly kind of sorrow brings about a change of mind and life unto salvation, not to be regretted; but the worldly kind of sorrow produces death.

[11]For see, this very thing, the godly kind of sorrow that you experienced, how much zeal it has called forth in you—yet what self-defense, yet what indignation, yet what fear, yet what longing, yet what ardor, yet what punishment; in every respect you showed yourselves to be innocent in the matter.

[12]So even if I wrote you, it was not on account of the wrongdoer, nor on account of the one wronged, but that your devotion for us might be manifested to you in the presence of God.

[13]Because of this we have been comforted; and in our comfort we rejoiced the more exceedingly at the joy of Titus, since his spirit has been refreshed by you all.

[14]For if I have boasted about anything to him about you, I was not put to shame; but as we have spoken everything to you in truth, so also our boasting before Titus was truth.

[15]And his affections are the more abundantly toward you, as he recalls the obedience of you all, as with fear and trembling you received him.

[16]I rejoice that in everything I am able to depend on you.

7

Paul's Joy at the Response of the Corinthian Church

2 Corinthians 7:2-16

Verse 1 recalls the verses in chapter 6 that preceded it, namely, the call to the separate life and the promise of God to dwell in the midst of His people as the Father and in a relationship in which the people themselves are to be as sons and daughters. The verse could very well amount to an extention of chapter 6.

Now that we have these promises, dear friends, let us cleanse ourselves from all defilement of body and spirit, perfecting our holiness in the fear of the Lord (v. 1).

The word "cleanse" is from an old word in the New Testament which meant, as in John 15:2 to *prune*. In the old inscriptions it was used for ceremonial cleansing. The cleansing process was a voluntary matter, and Paul's use of the aorist subjunctive suggests that the process is something that is to be done—completed once and for all. Notice that Paul said, "Let us," which included himself in the admonition. The word "defilement" carried the ancient meaning to stain, to pollute. It is a broad coverage for all kinds of filthiness of the flesh as well as moral, mental, and ceremonial filthiness. The words "perfecting our holiness" indicate a method that is "aggressive and progressive." It is something that continues to go on in the life of the believer. A kind of holiness of which Paul spoke is marked by a process that is continuous (1 Thess. 3:13; Rom. 1:4). The whole atmosphere of Corinth, and many of the people in the church, indicate that these were just the people to receive this admonition. There was perhaps not another city in world where there were more degrading life-styles and counteracting types of immorality than were to be found in Corinth. Paul's words of "body and spirit" are to remind the Corinthians that good and bad are found operative in the two spheres of man's existence, "the biological and intellectual," as Jean Herring put it. Paul wanted holiness to be brought to its finest flower in the lives of the Corinthians. Of course, this stage of development is not possible through human effort alone; it is a cooperative matter in which a person does his best while putting his trust in God completely and his dependence on Him fully. And all of this is to be brought about "in the fear of the Lord." And what does the fear of the Lord mean? It means the disposition on the part of the believer to give God the respect that is due him as Creator and as Savior and never to lose sight of the fact that there is a final day in which every person is to be judged according to one's deeds, whether good or bad, and that there will likewise be a final separation of "the sheep and the goats" (Matt. 24).

1. A Plea for Acceptance and Understanding (vv. 2-5)

Make room for us (in your hearts); we treated no one unjustly, we corrupted no one, we took advantage of no one (v. 2).

The words "make room for us" come from an old world meaning place, as to leave space or provide a space for someone or something. Paul confronted the Judaizers face to face. He sought to set at rest any disposition on the part of anyone to condemn him whether in the matter of doctrine, morals, or money. There had been no improper conduct on his part, for he had shown his painstaking regard for the rights of all. (One could take the words "make room for us" to mean merely to understand us. But I prefer to take the word with its original meaning "to make room.") Paul's words were indeed apt as guidelines for all Christian workers and for all the ministers of the gospel. And to implement these words certainly requires an ardent effort on the part of the minister to keep on perfecting his "holiness in the fear of the Lord" (v. 1). If this had been scrupulously done by all of the evangelists in our day, the religious scandals that had plagued the body of the church and which have caught the unfavorable eye of such vast segments of the media, could not have taken place. Certainly, no minister of the gospel lives to himself or dies to himself. Whether in life or in death he is the Lord's minister and must ever regard himself as such.

I say this not to condemn, for I told you before that you are in our hearts to die together and to live together (v. 3).

Paul did not want the Corinthians to feel that he was pointing a condemnatory finger at any one or any group of them in particular at this point. Apparently he was not alluding to persons as such. Surely there were many in the church, as he had pointed out in his first letter to the Corinthians, who behaved improperly. But at this point Paul spoke from a higher plane of communication. Evidently he was trying to help the Corinthian Christians to understand more clearly the true bond of fellowship, the unalloyed union between himself and the Christian Corinthians. Such a union bears the seal of the Holy Spirit, God's definitive promise that the blessings of the Spirit's presence are not to be compared, except in kind, with the multiplied blessings of the Spirit for the believer at the last day. It is this concept of the spiritual bond that is to motivate the loyalty of believers, both to God and to mankind, not merely the thought of right and wrong whose consequences must be kept in view forever. This bond amounts to a cemented relationship that continues whether by death or by life. It is a spirit of togetherness that death cannot erase. This is the mood, or spirit, that needs to be recalled by every Christian in the contemporary church. There needs to be more of the spirit of *togetherness,* more consciousness of the bond of unity and of endearment that God expects His children to enjoy in their daily contacts of life. Actually, there appears to be on the part of some today more loyalty to the clubs to which they belong than to the church of which they are a member. People boast, and so do the clubs, of the perfect attendance record of the members. How often do we hear such boasting of attendance loyalty to the church?

Great is my boldness in speech toward you; great is my pride

in you. I am filled with encouragement; I am overflowing with joy in all our affliction (v. 4).

Paul expressed, in a very touching way, his feelings concerning the response of the Christians of Corinth to his efforts as an apostle. His words indicate that he was all but overcome with emotion and feeling concerning the Corinthian church. Filled with pride in the Corinthians, and with encouragement he had been bold in his speech toward them. He had held back nothing as he counseled with them and urged them to implement in their lives the intended life-style of God's divine expectation of them. He wanted them, as Peter would say, simply to endeavor to follow in Christ's steps in all their ways. After all, it was Christ who left the *copybook* as a role model for them to write their lives by, and Paul would take no credit for the glory of their achievement. He did acknowledge that the good news that came to him concerning the conduct of the Corinthian Christians had brought to his heart a joy that was simply "overflowing." This joy was so constant and real that the afflictions he had suffered were unable to cancel it. Paul's joy was so great that by analogy it might be likened unto the floodwaters of a mighty river overflowing its banks and depositing rich layers of alluvial soil on the neighboring fields. Paul's troubles were by no means over, but his comforting thoughts and his consolation would ever be with him in life and in death.

> **For even when we arrived in Macedonia our body had no relief; rather we were afflicted on every side—strife without, fears within (v. 5).**

The buffeting experiences of Paul left their marks upon his body. After all, he had suffered physical violence at the hands of his adversaries. He was "afflicted" on every side. There were the "strife without, fears within." The tense efforts of his adversaries to denegrate his mission and cut him short of his objective affected him both physically and mentally. For that matter, who has a mind so strong and so detached from actual life situations as not to be perturbed by such experiences as Paul had? The references here suggest the general impact of all the disagreeable aspects of life with which Paul was confronted at the hands of his adversaries. It all amounted to daily circumstances from which he had no complete deliverance.

2. The Coming of Titus (vv. 6-8)

> But God, who comforts the lowly, comforted us in the coming of Titus, and not only by his presence but also with the encouragement with which he was encouraged by you, as he reported to me your longing for me, your mourning, your warmth of feeling for me, so that I rejoiced still more (vv. 6-7).

The coming of Titus with the good news, however, had brought to Paul immediate comfort. He was especially encouraged by the Corinthians' reception of Titus and by his words concerning their longing for Paul. Evidently Titus had not only a perceptive mind but also an unusual ability to interpret for Paul the true mind of the Corinthians. As the go-between Titus understood the rich emotions of the Corinthians and the depth of their feeling for Paul and was able to translate those deep feelings of regard in such a way as to bring God's comfort to Paul. Evidently the letter referred to in verse 8 had already arrived at Corinth before Titus left; if so, the Corinthians must have received it with cordial understanding. It had accomplished what Paul wanted it to accomplish. Therefore, when Titus came with the good news about the situation in Corinth, it simply caused Paul to rejoice "still more." The response of the Corinthians portrayed a lovely picture of their regard for Paul, a picture in which there were not only tears of sorrow but also tears of gladness.

> For even if I offended you in the letter, I do not regret it; even if I did regret it (for I now see that the letter irritated you for only a short time) (v. 8).

In verse 8 Paul laid bare the thoughts of his heart in a very humane way. He confessed that he had no regrets in writing the letter, even though it may have offended the Corinthians. If he did once regret it, he soon came to understand that the irritation caused by the letter was of short duration. It was a matter that belonged to the past. It was the kind of thing that Paul was able to bury in an unmarked grave, for he had put it completely behind him.

The regretful mood that Paul had at first, as he thought of the letter and its effect on the Corinthians, soon gave way to gladness in the light of the meaningful prospect of the letter for the future of the Corinthians. After all, the irritating aspect of the letter lasted only for a brief season (literally, an hour). This kind of response to sharp words of reproof can logically take place only when the minds and hearts of the recipients are truly alert with spiritual purpose. The response is a good commentary on the growth and development of the spiritual insight of the Corinthians in relation to their spiritual counselor. There are those, even in a religious body, who are aversive to truth. Any kind of noxious stimuli, or anything associated with such, tends to abolish any ground for the desired response. At the bottom of it all, of course, is the wounded pride, the root of selfishness which, in reality, is the actual embodiment or personification of the uncontrolled ego.

3. Godly and Worldly Sorrow (vv. 9-12)

> Now I rejoice, not that you were humiliated, but that you became sorrowful enough to repent; for you became sorrowful as God would have it, in order that you might in no way suffer injury by us. For the godly kind of sorrow brings about a change of mind and life unto salvation, not to be regretted; but the worldly kind of sorrow produces death (vv. 9-10).

Paul distinguishes between two kinds of sorrow: "godly sorrow" and "worldly sorrow." These two kinds of sorrow differ as does the night from the day. Godly sorrow, of course, is the sorrow that comes about *according to God*. It is sorrow that makes for repentance, a complete change in one's life-style, and in one's attitude toward God and persons. It is the kind of sorrow that motivates the individual to embrace, and to implement, a lifestyle that is in accord with God's commands. It is a change of mind and of heart that issue in godly conduct. Worldly sorrow, on the other hand, is an altogether different kind of sorrow. It is not unlike the kind of sorrow which a father manifested toward his son who had been caught by the law, saying, "I am not disciplining you for what you did, but for allowing yourself to get caught by the law." A worldly kind of sorrow is induced by selfishness, while the godly kind of sorrow brings out the unselfish mood, the disposition to accept and conform to the commands of God. The godly kind of sorrow brings about "a change of mind and life unto salvation," a kind of change that leaves no room for regrets. On the other hand, "the worldly kind of sorrow produces death."

So, here again Paul held up the alternatives of life and death, and the individual has to make the choice, no one else can make the choice. There is no suffragan, no auxiliary bishop for the soul. There is no surrogate to bear the burdens of the soul and handle them to benefit the future.

Esau had his tears and Judas had his remorse, but such in no way freed them from the consequences of their deeds. Are the contemporary churches losing sight of the theological implications bound up in these two verses of Scripture (vv. 10-11)? Is it possible that the life-style of so many confessed believers in the contemporary church is due to the fact that, as they profess a desire to begin their spiritual pilgrimage, they fail to have in their hearts godly sorrow for their past life? Did they lack a burning conviction that there had to be a change, a change accompanied not only by regret, but by decisive action that would be as lasting as life itself?

> **For see, this very thing, the godly kind of sorrow that you experienced, how much zeal it has called forth in you—yet what self-defense, yet what indignation, yet what fear, yet what longing, yet what ardor, yet what punishment; in every respect you showed yourselves to be innocent in the matter (v. 11).**

Paul did not imply here that the Corinthians were perfect in their life-style, but he did imply that they were making progress in their quest for the good life. And this one thing they did achieve: they dealt with the problem of incest in a worthy way. After all, incest was a particular sin for which the church as a whole could not be held responsible, so long as they dealt with the matter in a godly way. The Corinthians had been negligent in dealing with the open sin, though inwardly they opposed it. At least that must have been the observation and the conviction of Titus, who brought the report to Paul.

The word translated "innocent" is an old word used, among the various usages, for *a pure virgin*. This would indicate that Titus had brought to Paul a straight account of the problem and of the response of the Corinthians in dealing with it. Though the sinful act of one man left a saddening impact on the whole body of believer's the guilt of the church as a whole rested only upon the indecisive manner in which the problem was dealt with.

What would happen in churches today if there came to be worthy discipline of offending members whose offensive deeds have come to be known? What if there were loving discipline that would serve to clear the good name of the church and also cause a turn around on the part of the offending member? Are the churches as a whole guilty of great neglect in the respect?'

> So even if I wrote you, *it was* not on account of the wrong-doer, nor on account of the one wronged, but that your devotion for us might be manifested to you in the presence of God (v. 12).

4. Love and Joy (vv. 13-16)

Although the letter from Paul to the church had to deal incisively with the problem brought about by the wrongdoer, there was also a deep sense of love out of which the letter went. From his words Paul must have had a very deep sense of love for the Corinthians and a feeling of appreciation so great, because of their devotion to him, that he wanted that devotion to be "manifested to you in the presence of God." Perhaps the body of Christians that Paul loved most was the group that composed the Philippian church, but his love for the Corinthians in a different setting, was marked by genuine affection. The words of this verse reflect an intimate, personal relationship found only in the interrelationship of pastor and people. Some prefer to translate the words "to you" as being "with you" in the presence of God. But the ancient text is clear and means, I believe, "to you" as we have it here—"to you in the presence of God."

> **Because of this we have been comforted; and in our comfort we rejoiced the more exceedingly at the joy of Titus, since his spirit has been refreshed by you all (v. 13).**

There is an expression of a double sense of joy here, the joy of Paul that came as a result of the good tidings that Titus brought and the joy that Titus himself experienced at the hands of the Corinthians because of their warmhearted reception of him. Whatever other reactions Titus may have had concerning his visit at Corinth, he came away with a sense of encouragement and with a heart full of hope for them and for Paul in their future relationship. He had been "refreshed" by the Corinthians and joy had come to his heart and this, in turn, brought comfort and rejoicing, all the more, to the heart of Paul.

> **For if I have boasted about anything to him about you, I was not put to shame; but as we have spoken everything to you in truth, so also our boasting before Titus was truth (v. 14).**

Complicated as matters had been in Paul's dealing with the Corinthians by letter, there was nothing in it all to put him "to shame." On every occasion he had spoken plainly to the Corinthians in truth, and whatever boasting he had done about them likewise "was truth." Paul was no deceiver. There was no guile in him. When he spoke, he spoke from the heart of things as he saw them to be, and in accord with truth. There was no vanity in his words, nothing vainglorious. Paul had praised Timothy (1 Cor. 16:10) even as he had praised Titus. But he had no word to take back on the matter. His praise stood the test.

> **And his affections are the more abundantly toward you, as he recalls the obedience of you all, as with fear and trembling you receive him (v. 15).**

The stubborn minority at Corinth that still opposed Paul was unable to discredit and to rob Titus of his victory there. His victory was complete. Though he came to the Corinthians with a stern, cutting message and though they "trembled at his words" (Eph. 6:5; Phil. 2:12), yet they came, on the whole, to receive him gladly and with understanding. The word translated "affections" (v. 15) is the word used among the ancient writers to express the seat of tenderest emotions. It is the same word used by Matthew (9:36) when he described the inner feeling that Jesus had for the people to whom He was ministering, people who had been harassed and maltreated as sheep without a shepherd. And as Titus recalled the obedience of the Corinthians, his affection toward them was all the more. Some give the words "as he recalls" causal force but I believe it is well to translate the passage as we have it here, "As he recalls the obedience of you all. . . ."

I rejoice that in everything I am able to depend on you (v. 16).

Paul's rejoicing rested on his confidence in the Corinthians, and their response to his message made his confidence well-founded. His words were not based upon blind confidence. One can have blind confidence in God, in Christ, but not always in people, Christians though they be! For even so-called Christians at times become wild, whimsical, unpredictable, and erratic in their attitudes even toward truth; falling victims to the vagaries of circumstance.

¹Now we make known to you, brothers, the grace of God that has been given among the churches of Macedonia,

²how that, in much proof of affliction, the abundance of their joy and their deep poverty abounded unto the riches of their liberality;

³for they gave according to their ability, I bear witness, and near their capability, of their own accord,

⁴with much entreaty begging us for the favor of participation in the collection for the saints.

⁵This was not as we had expected. But first they gave themselves to the Lord and to us, through the will of God,

⁶so that we requested Titus that, just as he had made a beginning before, he would also complete in you this grace.

⁷Therefore just as you abound in everything—in faith and speech and knowledge, and in every kind of zeal, and in the love from us in you—see that you abound in this grace also.

⁸I speak not as a command, but as testing, through the zeal of others, the genuineness of your own love.

⁹For you know the grace of our Lord Jesus Christ, how that, being rich, yet for your sakes he became beggarly poor, that by his poverty you might become rich.

¹⁰And I give an opinion in this: that it is fitting for you who were the first to begin beforehand, a year ago, not only to do it, but also to will it.

¹¹Now you should finish the action also, so that just as there was the readiness to will so there may be also *the readiness* to complete the giving out of the means you have.

¹²For if the readiness is already there, it is acceptable according to what one has, not according to what he does not have.

¹³For this is not to make it difficult for you in order to relieve others, but as a matter of equality,

¹⁴that your abundance at this time may supply their need, and that their abundance may supply your need, so there may be equality;

¹⁵just as it is written: he that *gathered* much had no increase, and he who *gathered* little had no less.

¹⁶But thanks to God, who is continually giving the same zeal for your sake in the heart of Titus;

¹⁷for he indeed accepted our request and, being very earnest, he went forth of his own accord to you.

¹⁸And we have sent together with him the brother whose praise in the gospel *is manifest* through all the churches.

¹⁹And not only so, but he was chosen by the churches as our travel companion with this charitable act being ministered by us to the glory of the Lord and to show our good will,

²⁰avoiding this: that any one should blame us in this lavish gift which is ministered by us.

²¹For we have regard for what is good not only in the sight of the Lord but also in the sight of men.

²²And we have sent with them our brother whom we have tested in many ways, many times, and found to be zealous, and now even more zealous in his great confidence in you.

²³If there is inquiry about Titus, he is my partner and fellow-worker unto you, or about our brothers, they are messengers of the churches, the glory of Christ.

²⁴Show them therefore in the presence of the churches the proof of your love and of our boasting about you.

8

The Grace of Giving

2 Corinthians 8:1-24

We come now to what may be regarded as the second main thrust of the Epistle, namely, the collection among the Corinthian Christians on behalf of the poor Judean Christians. The collection had already been mentioned in 1 Corinthians 16:1, and apparently an effort was already underway to enlist the people in worthy giving in behalf of the poor saints at Jerusalem (see 2 Cor. 8:10; 9:2). Evidently the need there was great, and acute, and the matter had been on Paul's heart for a long while (Gal. 2:10). He addressed the matter realistically and called upon the Corinthians to do their best.

1. The Example of the Macedonian Churches (vv. 1-7)

Notice how the apostle began his appeal by holding up the example of the churches of Macedonia.

> **Now we make known to you, brothers, the grace of God that has been given among the churches of Macedonia, how that, in much proof of affliction, the abundance of their joy and their deep poverty abounded unto the riches of their liberality; for they gave according to their ability, I bear witness, and near their capability, of their own accord (vv. 1-3).**

Paul broke fresh ground here in referring to the offering as "the grace of God." He meant, of course, the offering of God that had already been given by the churches of Macedonia. But the apostle regarded the offering as an outpouring of God's grace and believed that this grace had been given among the churches of Macedonia. He placed the offering in behalf of the poor saints of Jerusalem on the lofty level where every church offering should be placed. First, the cause should be worthy. Second, the response should be the result of the grace of God at work in the hearts of the believers. As a pastor, I have often said that the annual "every-member canvass" was one of the most distasteful tasks of my ministry for this reason: if the professed followers of Christ elevated the matter of giving to the place it belongs in Christian theology, there would be no need for the annual every-member canvass, but only canvasses for special offerings that might deserve support from time to time. The giving of these Macedonian Christians was the fruit of the grace of God "given among the churches."

The word "grace" *(charis)* is the word from which we get our English words *charisma, charismatic* and that is what the giving among the Macedonian Christians amounted to: it was a charismatic experience. And while we are on this word *charisma* or *charismatic,* let me say that every born-again Christian, by divine intent, is a charismatic. That does not mean that he must speak in tongues or have an unusual outpouring of the Holy Spirit in his life apart from the outpouring that came upon him when he was born into the household of faith. If the believer is a growing Christian, constantly passing from the shallow waters into the deep waters of Christian experience, he will experience again and again great outpourings of the Spirit. This is a theological truth that ought to be emphasized and kept clear in the mind of every follower of Christ.

But notice the source of the offerings among the Macedonian churches. Christians were poor and had their afflictions. The people of Macedonia had known better days. There had been days when the nearby mining operations had brought to the people wealth and bounties beyond the ordinary. But this was a thing of the past, and now their poverty was much as is the poverty of abandoned mining camps where the source of the gain is gone and the people are left in an impoverished state to get along the best way they can. Paul was careful, and painted an accurate picture of the giving of these Christians. They gave "according to their ability," and not only that, they gave "near their capability," that is, near the very best they could do. They did this "of their own accord" (v. 3). Put this kind of giving alongside the giving of the average congregation among our contemporary churches and see what you find! Most of the giving in support of the church is the result of the offerings of not more than one third of the church members. Many of the members rarely give as much as a dime to the work. Some do not give at all. Some give because they are *canvassed and given a fresh reminder of their duty*. Who knows but what some of the giving is due to the matter of self-respect? But that is only for God to judge.

> **With much entreaty begging us for the favor of participation in the collection for the saints (v. 4).**

Notice that the initiative in the matter of the collection among the Macedonians was taken by them. They literally begged the apostle for an opportunity to share in the collection for the poor saints. This leads one to assume that Paul might have had some reticence in calling on the Macedonian Christians to share out of their meager resources in the effort to care for the poor Christians in Judea.

Here at least is an example that is worthy for all Christians to follow. They were poor, but their poverty was no drawback to their giving. As they were able they gave and their gifts almost matched their capability. One should not lose sight of the fact that in giving out of their poverty their joy abounded and made for even greater "riches of their liberality." But think about such members *begging for the privilege of giving* and especially when the offering was to be used only to help the poor away from home. Begging for such an opportunity? Whoever heard of such before?

> **This was not as we had expected. But first they gave themselves to the Lord and to us, through the will of God (v. 5).**

Here is the secret of this unusual point of liberality, the person's self-surrender to the Lord and to the work of His kingdom, "through the will of God." Their difficulties had been severe, and there was proof on every hand of their affliction; notwithstanding this fact, the amount of their offering must have been astounding. The Christians had no contingent bank accounts from which to draw, no surpluses or luxuries. They gave as the widow gave in Mark 12:41. Of course giving was not altogether spontaneous, one might say, since Paul took the initiative in apprising the Macedonians of the need. Nevertheless, they gave voluntarily. They were not pressured to give. They were not motivated by tear-jerking stories.

> So that we requested Titus that, just as he had made a be-ginning before, he would also complete in you this grace (v. 6).

The reference recalls an earlier visit by Titus. At any rate, the apostle desired that, after the offering at Corinth had been brought to a conclusion, all of the offerings from the churches could be taken together to Jerusalem in the ministry to the saints there.

2. The Supreme Test in Giving (vv. 7-8)

> Therefore just as you abound in everything—in faith and speech and knowledge, and in every kind of zeal, and in the love from us in you—see that you abound in this grace also (v. 7).

The apostle in these gripping words put the Corinthian Christians to the supreme test: "let your giving be on a par with your faith." The Macedonians gave according to their financial ability, and he would have the Corinthians give according to their theological knowledge and their spiritual zeal. He capped his argument by calling on the Corinthian Christians to give in accord with their love for God and for all who were ministers of His Word. Paul's words, "the love from us in you," probably served in a very ingenuous way to recall to their minds the part he had played in the development of this divine kind of love for the Lord and for one another.

> I speak not as a command, but as testing, through the zeal of others, the genuineness of your own love (v. 8).

What the apostle said here is not to be regarded as "an order" but rather as admonition and urgent appeal. The "zeal of others" means, of course, the example of others, namely, the Macedonians. It must have touched a tender spot in their minds at least when he said the response to the offering would be a test of "the genuineness" of their own love.

3. The Example of Jesus (v. 9)

For you know the grace of our Lord Jesus Christ, how that, being rich, yet for your sakes he became beggarly poor, that by his poverty you might become rich.

Here the apostle held up Christ as the supreme example in giving. See Paul's development of this same thought in Philippians 2:5-11. Notice the emphasis on Christ's poverty. Rich as He was by His endowments as God's only Son, and by His creative power, "he became" (literally made Himself) a beggar, so that by His example we might become rich in the realm of the spirit. In His preexistent state, before the incarnation, Christ did not look upon His riches as something to be "grasped" or held onto. Consequently He identified Himself completely with the people of the earth, taking upon Himself the human condition that enabled Him to be as one of the poorest of the poor. His sympathies are always evident for the poor. Why? Because they were "distressed and scattered as are sheep when they have no shephered" (Matt. 9:35f).

4. Readiness to Complete the Giving (vv. 10-12)

And I give an opinion in this: that it is fitting for you who were the first to begin beforehand, a year ago, not only to do it, but also to will it. Now you should finish the action also, so that just as there was the readiness to will so there may be also *the readiness* to complete the giving out of the means you have. For if the readiness is already there, it is acceptable according to what one has, not according to what he does not have.

Verse 10 has given translators a bit of difficulty, but it need not do so. What is meant by his words "it is fitting for you"? The words mean what they say in simple English. The Corinthian

Christians had started out to take the offering the year before, the first to begin that far in advance, but they had not completed taking up the offering. In the light of that, it was fitting that the Corinthians round out the effort by whatever means they might have. The apostle merely entreated the Corinthians to follow through in the matter which they had already begun the year before. To do such was a "fitting" thing, fitting for any body of believers.

All too often Christians stop an effort before the task is finished. Such failure takes place also in the material world. I knew a house, or rather the frame of a house, that stood beside the road between Traphill and North Wilkesboro, North Carolina, naked to the eye during the years of my childhood. As far as I know the house was never finished. In England they call such a failure "a folly." These words (vv. 11-12) are in a way a mixture of praise and admonition. The Corinthians had made the beginning, earlier than others, and for that they were due praise. But now they should complete the good work and do so according to their means, their ability. There is no pressure here for a big offering that might be used in comparison with other givers. But there is a thought here in verse 12 that needs to find a permanent resting place in the mind of every Christian in the matter of giving: "if the readiness is already there," the gift is acceptable to God when it is in accord with the ability of the giver. Each giver is to make his gift in accord with what he has, not in accord with what he does not have. There is nothing in Paul's words to imply that any human eyes of scrutiny will be looking over the giver's shoulder as he gives.

5. *The Principle of Equality (vv. 13-15)*

For this is not to make it difficult for you in order to relieve others, but as a matter of equality, that your abundance at this time may supply their need, and that their abundance may supply your need, so there may be equality; just as it is written: he that *gathered* much had no increase, and he who *gathered* little had no less.

Paul stressed the fact that this offering is in no way to create hardship on one to favor another. He held up rather as the ideal the matter of *fairness*, or "equality." The word "equality" comes from an old word *(isos)* which means *fair, equal*. This suggests the highest possible ideal in the matter of Christian stewardship. And in doing this, the apostle recalled Exodus 16:18, which reflected the strength of his words here, namely, the spirit of fairness and equality meeting the needs of the people. In gathering the manna in the desert, those who endeavored to gather more than they needed had nothing left over, while those who "gathered little had no less." Paul did not elaborate on the meaning of his words in verse 14. Did he mean to imply that the day might come when the Jerusalem Christians might have an opportunity to do for the Corinthians just what the Corinthians were now to do for them? Perhaps. At least this interpretation is possible.

6. *The Zeal of Titus and the Brother (vv. 16-19)*

> **But thanks to God, who is continually giving the same zeal for your sake in the heart of Titus; for he indeed accepted our request and, being very earnest, he went forth of his own accord to you (vv. 16-17).**

The apostle began to speak again concerning the mission of Titus. Notice that Paul was constantly putting "the same [kind of] zeal" on behalf of the Corinthians in the heart of Titus. But Titus did what he did because he was motivated to do so by God. The words "very earnest" simply mean that his conscientious concern for the cause was above the ordinary. Titus' zeal surpassed that of many others. Paul could hardly have given a more telling word of commendation in behalf of Titus concerning his response to Paul's request.

> **And we have sent together with him the brother whose praise in the gospel *is manifest* through all the churches. And not only so, but he was chosen by the churches as our travel companion with this charitable act being ministered by us to the glory of the Lord and to show our good will (vv. 18-19).**

"The brother," whoever he was, was a happy choice for the mission he was to go on. His good work was well known in the churches, and the praise for his work in "the gospel" was manifested "through all the churches." Moreover, the brother had been "chosen by the churches" for the mission. The word "chosen" is an old word that occurs only here in the New Testament and in Acts 14:23. The word (*cheirotonētheis*) literally means to choose or elect by raising the hands. The word is also used in the sense of *appoint* or *install*. Whether or not the brother was appointed by the raising of hands is not made clear in the Scripture.

7. Christian Ethics in Giving (vv. 20-21)

Avoiding this: that any one should blame us in this lavish gift which is ministered by us. For we have regard for what is good not only in the sight of the Lord but also in the sight of men.

Here is an obvious warning that might well be spread to all churches in the matter of the handling of money entrusted to the church's care for any and all purposes. The apostle was scrupulously careful that no one would have a basis for faultfinding in reference to the gift he ministered on behalf of the poor saints of Jerusalem. He declared the appearance of things relating to money should be "good not only in the sight of the Lord but also in the sight of men" (v. 21). Those handling church funds must see to it that there is not even the "semblance" of anything that is questionable. And remember, those who handle the money cannot be too careful.

8. Titus and Companions (vv. 22-24)

And we have sent with them our brothers whom we have tested in many ways, many times, and found to be zealous, and now even more zealous in his great confidence in you (v. 22).

It is interesting to note that the apostle does not mention this third brother by name. Why? No one knows. Some have surmised that the words "our brother" might indicate that he was a relative of the apostle. But I do not think this is true. Personally, I feel that, if the brother was a cousin or brother "according to the flesh," Paul would hardly have been willing for him to go as a messenger. Such might have detracted from his effort to keep everything free from criticism. Nepotism, favors bestowed on members of family relationships, is widespread in matters of government; but it should never occur in spiritual relationships. And when such relationships do occur, there should be no trace of nepotism in them. The church should have the same feeling about it. At any rate, this brother had been "tested in many ways, many times," and his zeal was even the more because of his confidence in the Corinthians.

> **If there is inquiry about Titus, he is my partner and fellow-worker unto you, or about our brothers, they are messengers of the churches, the glory of Christ (v. 23).**

In verse 23 no verb is expressed, but I supplied the word *inquire* so the passage reads, "if there is inquiry about Titus," for that is what is clearly implied by it, and in which there is no theological problem which surfaces in the translation. Paul gave his "partner and fellow-worker" all the praise that was needed and if any inquiry was made concerning "our brothers" Paul declared them to be messengers of the churches, the glory of Christ. The word "messengers" *(apostoloi)* comes from an old word *(apostellō)*, to send. They were looked upon as "messengers" but not necessarily in the same category as the twelve apostles.

> **Show them therefore in the presence of the churches the proof of your love and of our boasting about you (v. 24).**

Here we have a final admonition to the Corinthian church (and to churches in general) to treat with loving respect the messengers who come to them, in the name of Christ in the furtherance of the work of the kingdom. It is easy for a congregation of believers to become prosperous financially and to withdraw, as it were, into a shell of unconcern for causes that lie beyond the borders of their own immediate concern. But let every congregation remember this: when a church ceases to be missionary it dies. Let us add, it deserves to die.

[1]Now concerning the offering for the saints, it is unnecessary for me to continue to write to you,

[2]for I know your readiness which I boast about you to the Macedonians, saying that Greece has been prepared since last year and that your enthusiasm has stimulated the majority of them.

[3]But I have sent the brothers, lest our boasting about you should lose its justification, so that, just as I said, you may really be prepared.

[4]Otherwise, if Macedonians should come with me and find you unprepared, *we* (note that I say not *ye*) should be put to shame in this situation.

[5]I considered it necessary therefore to urge the brothers that they go on before unto you that they might make ready beforehand your afore-promised generous gift so it may thus be ready as a generous gift and not as a gift grudgingly given by niggardliness.

[6]But the point is this: he who sows sparingly will also reap sparingly, and he that sows generously will also reap generously.

[7]Each one just as he has made up his mind in his heart, is to give, not reluctantly, or from a sense of compulsion, for God loves one who gives cheerfully.

[8]For God is able to make all grace abound in you so that you, having always enough of everything, may abound in every good work;

[9]just as it stands written, "He has distributed; He has given to the poor; His righteousness abides forever."

[10]And He who provides seed for the sower, and bread for food, will provide and multiply your seed and will cause to increase the fruit of your righteousness;

[11]you will be enriched in everything unto all liberality, which produces through us thanksgiving to God.

[12]For the ministry of this kind of contribution not only supplies the needs of the saints but also overflows through their giving many thanks to God

[13]through the approved character of this contribution and praising God for the obedience of your confession of faith in the gospel of Christ and for the generosity of your contribution to them and to all.

[14]Meanwhile they themselves, also in prayer in your behalf, are longing after you because of the surpassing grace of God upon you.

[15]Thanks be to God for His indescribable gift.

9

The Offering for the Poor Saints at Jerusalem

2 Corinthians 9:1-15

Following his discourse on the grace of giving (2 Cor. 8:1-15) and his dialogue concerning Titus and his companions (vv. 16-24), the apostle Paul resumed his discussion about the offering for the poor saints at Jerusalem. Confident as he was in their "readiness" (v. 2) to give, he sent Titus and his companions on to Corinth to see that the collection was ready when he himself would arrive there. It may be surprising to see Paul resuming his exhortation here after his final words in chapter 8. But the exhortation was in order, for there were yet thoughts that had not been introduced in chapter 8. What he said in chapter 9 seems to follow quite naturally what he had said in chapter 8. The offering for the Jerusalem saints was evidently a prime objective of the apostle. Whether or not the offering would help to crystallize the affections of the Christians in Asia for their needy brothers in the Jerusalem area, Paul believed a viable faith should manifest itself in good works on the part of the believers. Not only this, but evidently the apostle wanted to strengthen the fellowship and the bonds of communication between the Christians in the various areas of his world. The sense of being God's fellow-workers was foremost in his thoughts. In fact, this was a manifest part of his doctrinal approach to the life-styles of his fellow Christians.

1. The Readiness of the Corinthians (vv. 1-5)

Now concerning the offering for the saints, it is unnecessary for me to continue to write to you (v. 1).

There may have been a good number of Paul's readers who agreed with this statement, for he had said much about giving in chapter 8. In fact, no other gospel writer dealt with the delicate subject of giving in such a forceful and complete way. His argument in chapter 8 became the classical basis for an appeal on giving for any group of Christians whether then or now. Nothing tells the story better than a good example of what the storyteller has in mind, and Paul found this example in the response of the Macedonian Christians. The impact of their example lives today and will continue to live wherever Paul's words are read and preached and translated into the life-style of Christians, however small the group or number may be. Some translators use the words "it is superfluous" instead of "it is unnecessary," but the meaning is much the same. The word Paul used simply indicates that he thought it was *needless, unessential,* for him to speak further on the matter of giving at that time. He stated in verse 2 quite clearly why he felt that way:

> **for I know your readiness which I boast about you to the Macedonians, saying that Greece has been prepared since last year and that your enthusiasm has stimulated the majority of them (v. 2).**

The apostle did not hesitate to let one church group know what another church group was doing in the matter of support for the offering that he was taking in behalf of the Jerusalem saints. Was this overt comparison designed to develop "healthy rivalry" among the churches? Hardly, in that sense of the word, if by rivalry we mean the work that marks the endeavor with the hope of boasting. In fact, this word that we translate "boasting" and "glorying" *(kauchaomai)* is a versatile word indeed. In the intransitive use, though, it means *to boast, to glory, to pride oneself* (Bauer), or *to take pride in a person or thing because of something.* The fact that the Christians of Corinth in the outlying reaches of the Christian community had been prepared for a year inspired others. Their zeal had "stimulated the majority of them." Here is a place where the hackneyed word *excite* can be used to advantage. The story of the zeal of the Corinthians, as well as the practical application of the zeal of the Macedonians, had excited other Christians. They were deeply stirred by the examples. But the apostle seemed to have had some reservations about how the preparations and the stirring resolves of a year before would be carried out without some further motivation:

> But I have sent the brothers, lest our boasting about you should lose its justification, so that, just as I said, you may really be prepared (v. 3).

The verb that Paul used here *(prepared)* is a perfect passive subjunctive, and this tends to place the matter in a nebulous cloud of uncertainty concerning the final issue of the offering. He wanted his words of glorying (boasting) to be fully justified, and the readiness to be complete in regard to the final roundup of the Corinthians' efforts in the collection.

> Otherwise, if Macedonians should come with me and find you unprepared, *we* (note that I say not *ye*) should be put to shame in this situation (v. 4).

Note that the word Paul used for "confident" (RSV) was a very old Greek word that from the days of Aristotle carried the notion of "substratum or foundation." Various examples of this usage are found in the ancient papyri. Some took the word translated "confident" to mean "in this matter" or "substance" or "supposition." But I believe the word "confident" expresses better the thought behind Paul's words. His boasting, his words of praise, were based upon his own confidence in what the Corinthians had already done and what they would eventually do as they completed their part in the giving effort. But I think Paul's words ("note that I say not *ye*") have their own thrust, the meaning of which the Corinthians could hardly have escaped. Paul felt that he had real grounds for hope that everything would end right, and he had been bold to express the grounds for it. Naturally, he wanted everything to turn out just as he had expected and as he had believed it would.

In these words the apostle touched on the failings of many Christians in the churches of our day. Many of them make pledges in good faith and with honest and sincere motives, but fail to carry through with them. Some could, but others could not, because of intervening circumstances which they failed to anticipate. For this reason pledge cards ought to carry the provision, maybe something like this: "God willing," "if Providence allows," or "if unforeseeable circumstances do not forbid." For instance, a man may make a pledge to his church for a given sum over the space of one to three years. It is altogether possible that a situation may develop which deprives him of carrying out his gracious intent. Once I knew a man stricken to death, lying in a hospital bed, and full of lament because of his terrible financial plight. His words were: "This illness, and these mounting costs, have taken away every dollar of my savings . . . I have utterly nothing left!"

> **I considered it necessary therefore to urge the brothers that they go on before unto you that they might make ready beforehand your afore-promised generous gift so it may thus be ready as a generous gift and not as a gift grudgingly given by niggardliness (v. 5).**

What Paul must have had in mind here was the kind of gift that carries a blessing with it, and for the gift to be a gift of blessing it must spring from a heart of blessing. On the other hand, there is a type of gift that comes from a miserly or stingy person, a person who is reluctant to give and what he gives he does without real generosity or in a small or scanty measure. Such giving is penurious, tight, miserly, avaricious, illiberal, mercenary. Evidently the Corinthians had promised in advance that they would make a "generous gift" and that was all that Paul asked for. How would Paul's words in verse 5 apply to the average giver in the churches of today? How many of the givers would be characterized, in the light of the gifts, as a person who is stingy, miserly, tight, close? That is a question that the individual needs to answer only to God, for it is before God that all will stand at the last day, not before man, for evaluation.

2. Sowing and Reaping (vv. 6-11)

> **But the point is this: he who sows sparingly will also reap**

> sparingly, and he that sows generously will also reap gener-
> ously (v. 6).

The word translated "generously" recalls the word "generous" in verse 5. It is an old word *(eulogia)* which carries the idea of *praise, blessing,* especially when used of the activity of God or of a benefit that was bestowed by God or Christ. It was used also in the sense of *consecration.* Since the use of the word invariably carried the concept of blessing, there developed the idea of *bounty,* hence the word *generous,* as a generous gift. Now a generous person is one who in giving or in sharing reflects the mood of unselfishness. Thus the expression, "a generous patron of the arts," meaning a person who has given liberally to support the arts. Such giving is magnanimous.

> **Each one just as he has made up his mind in his heart, is to give, not reluctantly, or from a sense of compulsion, for God loves one who gives cheerfully (v. 7).**

Reflected in this verse is something of the mood of verses 5 and 6, especially verse 6, where Paul employed a well-known principle in agriculture. To have a good crop, the sower must not sow scantily. This would be especially true in the planting and harvesting of rice in the Far East, where rice plants are set by hand in the well-watered ground, a laborious task, but one that yields a great harvest. The more the plants, the greater the harvest. Here the giver is encouraged to make up his own mind about the matter, to make it up "in his heart" and give accordingly. There is to be no reluctance about it, no feeling that he is giving because of a feeling of compulsion, as if it were something that he just had to do! It is interesting to note here that the word Paul used for our word "cheerfully" is an old Greek adjective *(hilaros)* which means, when used of things, *glad, cheerful.* From this same old word we derive our English word *hilarious,* which, of course, means *cheerful* and sometimes *boisterously merry*. It carries the idea of something that arouses great merriment, as a "hilarious story." So the word *cheerfully* packs a lot of meaning, meaning that can truly issue into a joyful experience on the part of givers and may even justify a celebration that is holy and selfless when the spirit of generosity is such as to justify it.

> **For God is able to make all grace abound in you so that you, having always enough of everything, may abound in every good work; just as it stands written, "He has distributed; He has given to the poor; His righteousness abides forever" (vv. 8-9).**

Paul called on Providence to witness. When the giver lives up to God's expectations and generously undertakes to do for God, in the matter of giving, what he feels God would have him to do, God follows with a miracle! Providence performs. It is a simple way to put it, but it is nevertheless fully true: generous giving makes for showers of blessings. Paul said that in this type of response on the part of donors God has the ability "to make all grace abound in you." The word "grace" *(charin)* comes from the word from which we derive our word *charismatic*. And there is a domino effect in this type of giving. Paul said: "so that you, having always enough of everything, may abound in every good work." Paul spoke of this kind of abundance in Philippians 4:13: "I have strength for all things in him who endues me with power." He carried the idea still further in verse 19: "And my God will supply liberally your every need according to his riches in glory in Christ Jesus." (See Ps. 112:9.) What else could a Christian want out of life than that which is promised in verses 8 and 9? After all, God's Word has reminded us that as persons we came into the world naked and that as persons we will go out of the world the same way, so far as material holdings are concerned.

Does the reader ever stop to think seriously on the fact that evening bell will soon ring for him and all of his possessions, all of his holdings, all of his lands, all of his cattle, all of his certificates of deposit, all of his values in stocks and bonds will pass to other hands? That is the way it is. One does not need to dwell upon this fact until one lives in a morose atmosphere—an atmosphere that is sullen and gloomy, fretful and peevish. On the other hand, the Christian who centers his thoughts and his affections on Jesus Christ has an opportunity to live in the spiritual realm in a spiritually lavish manner. Certainly, he can live in a cheerful spiritual atmosphere in Christ Jesus.

> And He who provides seed for the sower, and bread for food,
> will provide and multiply your seed and will cause to increase
> the fruit of your righteousness." Any temporal blessings that
> come to the believer are to be productive in the fruit of righ-
> teousness (v. 10).

Paul's words recall the words of the prophet Isaiah (55:10)
where "the rain will give seed to the sower and bread for food."
Note that the purpose of the bread and the food, and the multi-
plication of the seed, is to one end: "to increase the fruit of your
righteousness. In others words, the righteousness of God (v. 9) is
to make "the fruit" of righteousness on the part of God's children.

> You will be enriched in everything unto all liberality, which
> produces through us thanksgiving to God (v. 11).

Paul introduces another thought in verse 11: the liberal giving
of the Christian produces in the hearts of the givers "thanksgiving
to God." As the hymn goes, in this kind of giving, and along with
it, come "showers of blessings" from God, blessings that are en-
riching "in everything unto all liberality." But by all means the
mood of thanksgiving that is produced should not be overlooked, that of "thanksgiving to God." All of this recalls the original day of national Thanksgiving which sprang from the hearts of
the Pilgrim fathers in the first year of their harvest in the New
World. Notwithstanding the trials, the tribulations, and the shattering effects of illness and death, there burned brightly in their
hearts the mood of thanksgiving to God. It is of such thanksgiving that Paul spoke in these verses to the Corinthians. This offering in which the Corinthian Christians shared, along with other
churches, was not something that the donors had to do. They
had no outward compulsion, no obligation from the human
standpoint, to participate in the offering. It was purely a voluntary
matter in which the hearts of the givers were moved upon by the
Spirit of God.

3. The Ministry of Giving (vv. 12-14)

> For the ministry of this kind of contribution not only supplies
> the needs of the saints but also overflows through their giv-

ing many thanks to God through the approved character of
this contribution and praising God for the obedience of your
confession of faith in the gospel of Christ and for the generosity of our contribution to them and to all (vv. 12-13).

Paul applied the purely practical to the purely spiritual in these
verses. The practical side of it issues in only what will help to care
for the material needs of the poor saints of Jerusalem, while the
spiritual side of the activity "overflows through their giving many
thanks to God." So, in the giving of gifts and the ministry of the
gifts, which take place on the high level held up by Paul in reference to the offering, the blessings that come from the effort overflow in all directions. He urged the Christians themselves to
glorify God and manifest beyond all doubt their complete response to the challenge of the gospel of Christ. Such giving as
Paul referred to has met the test of God's will, a character that is
"approved" in the matter of giving. This kind of contribution and
its ministry (v. 12) meets the practical need of the recipients, and
of the donors in that the action *overflows through their giving
many thanks to God*. Here the concept of *faith* and *works* which
James emphasized in such a telling way is beautifully illustrated.
Dr. A. T. Robertson stated the case well: "the breathren in Jerusalem will know by this collection that Gentiles make as good
Christians as Jews" *(in loco)*. A good amen can be said to this. It
can also be said that where there is the right kind of faith in the
hearts of believers, the right kind of works will follow. You cannot
separate the one from the other. If somehow it should become
possible (or, let us say, fully realized) for the mood of Paul's message concerning the offering for the saints at Jerusalem to become part and parcel of the minds and the hearts of present-day
givers in the churches of our land, there would doubtless come
about a transformation in the response of givers to *every worthy
opportunity* relating to the stewardship of substance.

> **Meanwhile they themselves, also in prayer in your behalf,
> are longing after you because of the surpassing grace of God
> upon you (v. 14).**

Paul closed his dialogue on giving with some tender words that

have to do with "prayer," "longing." The words amount to a reference to closer ties of fellowship and genuine affection between
the Greeks and Judeans. There seemed to be in his words a
desire to bring together, as another has suggested, the Gentile-
Christians and the Judeo-Christians into more cordial relationship marked by genuine affection. There was the blessing that
came through the recipients in behalf of their benefactors who, all
the while, would be longing to see them "because of the surpassing grace of God" that rested upon Paul and those who shared
with him in the offering. This was in itself the result of God's grace
at work in the hearts of His people.

4. Paul's Joy (v. 15)

Thanks be to God for His indescribable gift.

What a burst of happiness, what an expression of joy, flowed
from the pen of the apostle in his closing words. The joy in it all,
and the feeling of thanksgiving, was beyond measure for God's
"indescribable gift." Here for once the apostle "wanted for words."
When he thought upon the character of God's gift in bringing
about these spiritual relationships between Gentile-Christians
and the Jewish Christians, and the growing bond of affection that
would flower into its finest form through the collection, he simply
could not describe it all. It was filled with "wonder beyond description" (Robertson).

2 CORINTHIANS 10

¹Now I, Paul, personally appeal to you by the gentleness and graciousness of Christ, I who face to face with you am indeed lowly among you, but when absent I am bold toward you;

²yes, I beg you that I may not when present be bold with the same confidence with which I plan to be bold against certain persons who look upon us as having a life-style according to the flesh.

³For though we live in the flesh, we do not serve in the army according to the flesh.

⁴For the weapons of our warfare are not of the flesh, but mighty with God to the destruction of fortresses, demolishing sophistries

⁵and every exalted thing that rises up in opposition to the knowledge of God, and taking captive every thought to subject them to Christ,

⁶and being ready to punish every disobedience, whenever your own obedience is brought to completion.

⁷Look at the facts before you: If anyone believes in himself that he is Christ's, he is to consider this again; for just as he is Christ's, so are we also.

⁸For if I should boast somewhat more abundantly about the authority which the Lord gave for building you up and not for tearing you down, I shall not be put to shame,

⁹lest I should seem as one who would terrify you by letters;

¹⁰for his letters, they say, are heavy and strong, while his bodily presence is weak and his speech amounts to nothing.

¹¹Such a person is to consider this: that whatever kind of person we are in word through letters when we are away, of such also indeed are we when we are present.

¹²For we dare not class or compare ourselves with anyone, commending some of those who commend themselves; rather those who measure themselves by themselves *do* not have understanding.

¹³But we will not boast beyond the limits, but by the measure of the standard which God measured out to us, to come also unto you.

¹⁴For we are not overextending ourselves, as though not coming to you, for we were the first to come to you with the gospel of Christ.

¹⁵For we do not boast beyond the limits in the labors of others, but have hope that as your faith increases we will be magnified in your sight according to our standard of measurement unto greater abundance,

¹⁶so as to preach the gospel even unto lands beyond you and not to glory in another's province with regard to the readiness of things.

¹⁷He who boasts is to boast in the Lord.

¹⁸For it is not the one who commends himself who is approved, but he whom the Lord commends.

10

Paul's Defense of His Ministry

2 Corinthians 10:1-18

In chapter 10, there is almost an abrupt change in Paul's dialogue with the Corinthian church. He has put behind him the matter of the collection for the poor saints of Jerusalem which he dealt with so fully in chapters 8 and 9. C. K. Barrett calls the break "a new division of the epistle," and in many respects it is all of that. After much waiting, the apostle began to defend his ministry and to deal boldly with those who differed with him. The group of dissidents, of course, embraced those who had led them astray—the false apostles who infiltrated the body of believers with their "different gospel" and their "other Jesus." They were the real seducers who endeavored to drive a wedge between Paul and the Corinthians. Then there were the recognized apostles and the tension that existed between them and the apostle Paul. In his confrontation with these various elements of dissension, Paul became completely forthright in his words of defense.

1. A Personal Appeal (vv. 1-2)

Now I, Paul, personally appeal to you by the gentleness and graciousness of Christ, I who face to face with you am indeed lowly among you, but when absent I am bold toward you (v. 1).

His opening words suggest, as A. T. Robertson noted, "at this point it is possible that Paul 'took the pen from the amanuensis' and wrote himself as he did in Galatians 6:11." At any rate the Judaizers in Corinth, though a minority group, had made accusations that upset him greatly, and he had to deal with the issue openly. There is no way to determine the exact character of the

119

accusations of this small group of people who opposed Paul. The thought in verses 1 and 2 is a bit difficult to unravel, but apparently the critics had accused him of being a two-faced person— that is, one kind of person when he was in their midst and another when he was away. In verses 10 and 11 this facet of the accusers is laid bare and so are Paul's words of defense.

Paul introduced his defense by appealing to the example of Christ, to whom he was committed so fully and by whose example he sought to live. Jesus, who was Himself a meek person (Matt. 11:29), one who exemplified the quality of meekness, spoke with words of praise for the meek (5:5). Among the Greek ethicists, a meek man was a man who knew how far to go and when to stop in dealing with his own rights. His attitude was marked by what Matthew Arnold called "sweet reasonableness." The word Paul used for "gentleness" *(prautētos)* was a word commonly used among the ancient Greeks for a wild beast that had become domesticated. The term came to mean, for the Christian, complete submission to the mind and will of God. Paul would make his appeal therefore on the basis of the "gentleness and graciousness of Christ." The implication here would be that the apostle had at least a hope that the Corinthians, in their response to his words, would act accordingly.

Evidently the dissenters had openly criticized Paul for being one thing when he was in their midst and another when he was away from them. In others words, they must have accused him of saying through letters what he would not have said had he been face to face with them when he would present himself as one "lowly among you." The word *lowly* as used by Aristotle and Socrates conveys the idea of "littleness of soul." Literally, the word *(tapeinos)* conveyed the idea of being *poor, of low position, undistinguished, of no account;* in a bad sense, it meant one who was subservient, pliant, humble, lowly. However the critics, in their words about Paul, evidently reflected a sneer, and Paul simply could not allow such degenerating references to him to go by without defense.

> **Yes, I beg you that I may not when present be bold with the same confidence with which I plan to be bold against certain**

persons who look upon us as having a life-style according to
the flesh (v. 2).

These words, *life-style according to the flesh,* must have stung
Paul severely. That was the last thing he would have wanted anyone to say about him. Actually his conduct on his three missionary journeys and his deportment in every bitter human situation
that arose reveal none of the aspects of a life-style that is "according to the flesh." Such words are damaging to the character of a
good man, especially to a minister of the gospel. One can only
surmise what the sneering adversaries had in mind in attacking
Paul with words such as these. Certainly they had no basis on
which to charge him of immorality. Did they wish to imply that
the wisdom to which he laid claim was "worldly"? Did they want
to charge him with a worldly approach, from an ethical standpoint, in all of his relationships with the Corinthians and other
churches? Of course, the answer to these questions cannot be
given; but even the casual observer, in reading the letters of the
apostle, could hardly be brought to feel that he was a man who
was self-assertive and who intended to be authoritarian in any
measure in dealing with those to whom he ministered whether at
Corinth or elsewhere.

2. The Spiritual Warfare (vv. 3-10)

For though we live in the flesh, we do not serve in the army
according to the flesh. For the weapons of our warfare are
not of the flesh, but mighty with God to the destruction of
fortresses, demolishing sophistries (vv. 3-4).

The warfare in which the apostle was engaged was a warfare
projected by the minds and hearts of men. In a certain sense it
was a battle with the brains of his accusers. These "certain persons" to whom he referred certainly set them apart from the body
of believers as a whole. Paul was not indicting the entire church,
nor was he replying to every church member except as they
might have been influenced by the false witnesses. At any rate he
wanted the Corinthians to distinguish between the things that differed in his warfare and the common warfare that has been the

nemesis of peace throughout the centuries. The real nemesis of peace is found in the perverted thoughts of mankind. Paul's campaign for Christ was of course nonmilitary. His weapons were not the conventional weapons of mankind, but spiritual weapons that were "mighty with God," so mighty that they were able to destroy the fortresses of man's design that were intended to hinder the progress of the gospel and to demean its character. The weapons Paul used were able to penetrate the shields of fallacious reasoning on the part of his opponents and to demolish fortresses erected by the false reasoning approaches of men who would like to destroy not only the character of the mission of God's ambassadors, but also the messengers themselves. Whatever the wily thoughts of worldly men might be, and whatever citadels their fallacious reasoning might erect, they were not, in all of their combined strength, sufficient to withstand the spiritual weapons of the apostles of Christ. Their weapons are weapons of the kind of power that is of God.

> **And every exalted thing that rises up in opposition to the knowledge of God, and taking captive every thought to subject them to Christ (v. 5).**

Paul's argument explains in a further way the character of the warfare in which he was engaged. The adversary was any and every "exalted thing" that rose up "in opposition to the knowledge of God." The battle that was going on at the moment was a battle of the minds of men, men who were assaulting the spiritual character of the witness of the apostle, as well as his moral character. One cannot attack the thoughts of a person without attacking his moral character, for the mind and the heart are as one. "As a man thinks in his heart, so is he" (Prov. 23:7). The apostle's warfare therefore was designed to take captive "every thought" with a view to subjecting those thoughts to Jesus Christ.

The early Christians were taught to do just this—subject themselves completely to the will of God. This is why James decried arrogant boasting (4:13-15): "Come now," he said, "you who say, 'Today or tomorrow we shall go into this city and spend a year there and carry on business and prosper'—you who indeed do not know the tomorrow or what kind of life is yours. For you are a vapor that is for a little time appearing, and then disappearing; instead of this, you are to say, 'If the Lord will, we shall both live and to do this or that.'" And this is why the early Roman Christians came to use so often the expression "God willing" *(Deo Volente)*. Paul knew, as all men must know, that when one takes the thoughts of any man, he has made a captive out of that man. This is what Paul wanted to do, make them captives of Christ. The power center of every man's force is his thoughts, his reasoning power. But Paul knew, and he would have all to know, that the power of the gospel sprang not from the force of human reasoning, but from the wellsprings of the revelation of God. Paul's own message as an apostle was a message from God that came to him as God's instrument of proclamation. And the man who is God's messenger today must at least have such a conviction if his words are to carry the persuasive power.

And being ready to punish every disobedience, whenever your own obedience is brought to completion (v. 6).

Paul's words at this point were incisive. He was ready for such acts of disobedience to be punished, but there appears a contingency in his readiness: "whenever your own obedience is brought to completion." These words seem to express Paul's desire to see the church as a whole become more obedient to Christ. Then the full round of any act of discipline could be more appropriately taken and fittingly observed. In others words, obedience on the part of all of the believers ought to be brought to a greater stage of maturity. And in his visit to Corinth Paul would expect to find greater loyalty on the part of the membership to him personally in his ministry there.

Look at the facts before you: If anyone believes in himself that he is Christ's, he is to consider this again; for just as he is Christ's, so are we also (v. 7).

The word *look*, "look at the facts before you," can be regarded as an imperative or as indicative. In other words, the passage can be translated, "you look at the facts," or "look at facts before you."

I prefer to take the words as an imperative. Paul wanted them to face up to the situation as it was. What were the facts? The facts were that the critics who regarded themselves as being truly Christian needed to take another look at things. They needed to realize that they had no "corner" on Christ; they did not have any special relationship to Him; for Paul himself belonged to Christ, and he was Christ's apostle called by Him and annointed by the Spirit for his mission. In 1 Corinthians 1:12, there is an allusion to a "Christ's party." Could there be an echo of that thought here? Of course the reference here could be to the Gnostics, who regarded themselves as the recipients of a special revelation from God.

> **For if I should boast somewhat more abundantly about the authority which the Lord gave for building you up and not for tearing you down, I shall not be put to shame, lest I should seem as one who would terrify you by letters; for his letters, they say, are heavy and strong, while his bodily presence is weak and his speech amounts to nothing. (vv. 8-10).**

Paul defended his role as an ambassador of Christ in no uncertain words. His mission was given him by the Lord for the purpose of building up believers and not "for tearing . . . down" as his critics had been attempting to do. So far as his letters were concerned, Paul disclaimed any disposition to frighten or terrify the recipients; and certainly, in the light of his messages to them, he had no fear of being "put to shame." The ground Paul stood upon was solid and every aspect of disobedience on the part of the Corinthian Christians was dealt with on the basis of established facts. They knew what had been going on and what was going on then, and Paul had full confidence in every phase of the report that Titus brought to him from Corinth.

The New Testament does not deal with the personal appearances of persons. The only reference that we have to Jesus in this respect is the fact that He "grew in stature and in wisdom" (Luke 2:52). Tradition, however, has not been too kind to Paul. An account in the second century from the *Acts of Paul and Thecla* pictured Paul as "small, short, bow-legged, with eyebrows knit together and an aquiline nose." None of that is here, but the smear is there just the same. They accused him as being heavy and strong in his letters, "while his bodily presence is weak and his speech amounts to nothing." They could hardly have been more unkind to Paul in their reference to his presence. Paul answered the shattering criticism, reminding them in simple words that the person whose word came to them through letters, when he was away, was to be regarded as the one and the same person when he was in their misdt. He lived no double life, and there was no two-faced character about him. The preacher they heard proclaiming his message in Corinth was no different from the apostle from whom they had received letters.

3. Invidious Comparisons (vv. 11-18)

> Such a person is to consider this: that whatever kind of person we are in word through letters when we are away, of such also indeed are we when we are present. For we dare not class or compare ourselves with anyone, commending some of those who commend themselves; rather those who measure themselves by themselves *do* not have understanding (vv. 11-12).

Paul was unsparing in his words of self-justification here; also he was unsparing in his words concerning those who commend themselves. The problem with them lay in the fact that they "measure themselves by themselves" and they do this without understanding. Paul said, in effect, that the Judaizers set their own standard of measurement and the standard was found in themselves—an arrogant assumption. Such a position recalls words of the Scottish poet, "O, wad some Power the giftie gie us To see ourselves as ithers see us!" Actually, the standard to go by is not the standard set by others. The only standard for the Christian is set by God. Maxims must come from Him if they are to be worthy.

> But we will not boast beyond the limits, but by the measure of the standard which God measured out to us, to come also unto you. For we are not overextending ourselves, as though not coming to you, for we were the first to come to you with the gospel of Christ (vv. 13-14).

Here Paul firmly declared that his standard of measurement was the standard of God with the sole purpose of reaching out unto the Corinthians. Paul was not pushing himself "forward" in any way or endeavoring in any measure to gain favor or acclaim for himself. Whatever his words of boasting were, that is, his glorying, it was not beyond the authority granted him by God in his call. He was the Apostle to the Gentiles, and any position that he had taken with reference to the saints of Corinth was within the scope of the authority that God had bestowed upon him in his call to the ministry. He had in no sense overextended himself. He was merely carrying out what he believed to be the mandate of God.

> **For we do not boast beyond the limits in the labors of others, but have hope that as your faith increases we will be magnified in your sight according to our standard of measurement unto greater abundance, so as to preach the gospel even unto lands beyond you and not to glory in another's province with regard to the readiness of things (vv. 15-16).**

Paul was the founder of the church at Corinth. None of his boasting or glorying concerning the work there had to do with the labors of others. Moreover, there was no intrusion on his part on the works of others in Corinth. In fact, he had taken advantage of the work of no one in order to boast. But Paul did express the hope that in the progress of the faith of the Corinthians they might come to have a deeper appreciation of his labors according to his standard of measurement. He had been completely within his rights in all that he had said about the work and his own labor in Corinth. But the real objective was not that he might have greater appreciation on the part of the Corinthians, but that their faith would make for the enlargement of their own witness to such an extent that the gospel would be preached far beyond their own borders. This is what Paul's "standard of measurement" called for, the rule by which he worked. He looked beyond, to other lands, where the gospel might be planted. He was aware that any accomplishment on his part, in his labors for God, was possible because of a divine "readiness of things" where God had moved before him in preparation for his coming. Such was a part of the destiny for which he longed. That was his standard of measurement, his divine maxim.

There was an obvious disposition on the part of Paul to blaze new paths for the gospel and to plant the good seed in soil that had not been planted before. There was nothing unworthy in that motive. Against this view is the disposition of believers to achieve, by a type of competition that seeks rank and status that surpasses others.

> **He who boasts is to boast in the Lord. For it is not the one who commends himself who is approved, but he whom the Lord commends (vv. 17-18).**

In bringing his discussion to a close concerning his defense of his own ministry, the apostle spoke from the mountaintop of excellency. If any boasting is to be done, it is to be done "in the Lord." If any commendation is to come, it is to come from the Lord. Any approval, any qualifying words concerning one's fitness for service and character of service, has viable meaning only if the approval comes from God. Only He who created the messenger, called him to service, and made him "fit" for that service can afford any grounds to boast. Every one of us who professes to be an ambassador of Christ might well display these two verses (vv. 17-18) in a suitable place on the desk of our study table or upon the wall above the desk, where they might be frequently seen as a motto for all life's work in the Lord.

¹O that you could put up with a little of my nonsense! At least do bear with me.

²For I am deeply concerned about you with godly concern; for I betrothed you to one husband, so as to present you to Christ a pure virgin.

³But I fear lest, in some way as the serpent led Eve astray by his trickery, your thoughts have been corrupted from their sincerity (and purity) in Christ.

⁴For if indeed the one who comes preaching any other Jesus whom we did not preach, or a different Spirit which you did not receive, or another gospel which you did not accept, you rightly hold yourselves erect and steadfast.

⁵For I consider myself to have been in no way inferior to the super-apostles;

⁶and even if I am untrained in speaking, to the contrary, I am not in knowledge, having made this plain to you in every respect, in all things.

⁷Or did I commit a sin in humbling myself that you might be exalted, since I preached God's gospel to you free?

⁸I robbed other churches, accepting material support for service to you.

⁹And when I was present with you, and in need, I was not a burden to anyone; for the brothers who came from Macedonia supplied my needs; and in everything I kept, and I will keep, myself from being a burden to you.

¹⁰Because Christ's truth is in me, this boasting shall not be stopped in me in the entire regions of Achaia.

¹¹Why? Because I do not love you? God knows.

¹²But what I now do, that I will keep on doing, that I may cut off the opportunity of those desiring an occasion to the end that in their boasting they may be found to be just as weak as we are.

¹³For such men are false, deceitful workmen transforming their appearance into apostles of Christ.

¹⁴And no wonder, for Satan himself changes himself into an angel of light.

¹⁵It is no great thing therefore if his servants disguise themselves as servants of righteousness, whose end will be according to their works.

¹⁶Again I say, no one is to consider me to be foolish, but if not, receive me as foolish that I also may boast a little.

¹⁷What I am saying now, I speak not according to the Lord, but as in foolishness in this confidence of boasting.

¹⁸Since many boast according to the human point of view, I will also boast.

¹⁹For gladly you who are wise put up with the foolish ones.

²⁰For you put up with it if anyone enslaves you, if anyone strips you of your possessions, if anyone takes you captive, if anyone puts on airs, if anyone strikes you in the face.

²¹I speak to my shame, as though we have been weak; but in whatever way anyone would be bold (I speak foolishly) I am bold also.

²²Are they Hebrews? So am I. Are they Israelites? So am I. Are they the seed of Abraham? So am I.

²³Are they servants of Christ? (I am talking as one beside himself), I am more than they; I have been in difficulties far more, in prisons even more, in beatings beyond measure, at death's door many times.

²⁴Five times I received from the Jews forty lashes, less one;

²⁵three times I was beaten with rods, once I was stoned, three times I suffered shipwreck; I spent a day and a night adrift at sea;

²⁶In my journeys I was often in dangers from rivers, in dangers from robbers, in dangers from my family, in dangers from the Gentiles, in dangers in the city, in dangers in the wilderness, in dangers on the sea, in dangers among false brothers,

²⁷in labor and in hardship, in sleepless nights frequently, in famine and in thirst, in fastings often, in cold and in nakedness.

²⁸And apart from the things I omit, I had the daily pressures on me of anxiety about all churches.

²⁹Who is weak, and I am not weak also? Who is caused to stumble, and I am not inflamed?

³⁰If I must boast, I will boast about the things that relate to my weakness.

³¹The God and Father of our Lord Jesus, who is blessed forever, He knows that I am not lying.

³²In Damascus, the ethnarch under Aretos, the king, guarded the city of the Damascenes to arrest me,

³³and through a window I was let down in a basket through the city wall, and I escaped their hands.

11

Paul's Defense of His Ministry (cont.)

2 Corinthians 11:1-33

It was necessary for the apostle to continue in an even more forceful way, his self-defense against the little group of critics who tried to discredit the character of his apostleship and to talk down his work. His dialogue in verses 1-15 is merely a continuation of the defense which he put forth in the preceding chapter. It was hard enough merely to be criticized by his adversaries, but when they came they questioned the authentic character of his apostleship. That was just too much for him to let go by without answer. In these opening verses of chapter 11 he set forth some marks of the character of genuine apostleship and, in doing so, provided the readers with added insight concerning his own life.

1. A Slight Tinge of Apology (v. 1)

O that you could put up with a little of my nonsense! At least do bear with me.

Paul's opening words are a bit tantalizing. Although the words aroused interest in what he was about to say, verse 1 is difficult to follow. He expressed a wish about the present when he said "Oh that you could" *(ophelon)* and then followed the wish with the words "At least do bear with me." The verb he used can be taken as either the imperative middle or present middle indicative. I take it to be the imperative, meaning "do bear with me." There is almost a tinge of apology in his opening words which seem to deprecate his position which became clear as he went on with his defense.

2. Paul's Deep Concern for the Corinthians (vv. 2-4)

For I am deeply concerned about you with godly concern; for

130

> I betrothed you to one husband, so as to present you to
> Christ a pure virgin (v. 2).

The passage recalls the figure of Israel as a bride and Yahweh
as the bridegroom, a metaphor frequently used by the prophets
in the Old Testament. (See Isa. 54:5; 62:5, Hos. 2:19.) Paul
portrayed himself as the paranymph or friend of the bridegroom
(we say, groomsman) who accompanied the bridegroom when
he went to bring home his bride. Such a custom dated back to
the ancient Greeks. It is a fitting figure in that Paul was the
founder of the Corinthian church and the one who logically
would present the church to Christ. Paul was the path breaker of
the Christian witness in Corinth; and he had zealously endeavored to prepare the church for her role as a bride of Christ. A
godly jealousy swept over him as he thought of any digression on
the part of the church from that intended role.

> But I fear lest, in some way as the serpent led Eve astray by
> his trickery, your thoughts have been corrupted from their
> sincerity (and purity) in Christ (v. 3).

The analogy of the serpent and Eve in the Garden may be a bit
far-fetched, but the idea rings true. Any departure from God's
intended life-style for the Corinthians was brought about by Satan, the master deceiver. The church was young, a mere baby
trying to stand up and walk, and was therefore a choice target for
the deceptive wiles of the devil. Paul pleaded here for a genuine
sincerity of mind and heart on the part of the Corinthian church,
the kind that would allow for only singleness of affection. Any
other course on the part of the church would be spiritual fornica-
tion. Paul stated the grounds for his concern openly: it was his
anxiety concerning the possibility of their being seduced by the
trickery of the devil.

> For if indeed the one who comes preaching any other Jesus
> whom we did not preach, or a different spirit which you did
> not receive, or another gospel which you did not accept, you
> rightly hold yourselves erect and steadfast (v. 4).

There was to be no wavering, no letup in their doctrinal views.
In the ancient classical Greek this word *anechō* which Paul used

carried the idea of "hang together," and that would do for the meaning here. Paul did not want a single one of them to be swept away from the ideal of religious devotion to Christ according to the plain, simple gospel which he had preached to them. Whether or not one understands fully the figures employed by Paul in this verse to stress his point, the idea is clear: the Corinthians were to stand together and hold out against any type of heresy that might invade their ranks in an effort to insult the role of Jesus as Savior and Redeemer.

3. Paul and the False Apostles (vv. 5-15)

> **For I consider myself to have been in no way inferior to the super-apostles; and even if I am untrained in speaking, to the contrary, I am not untrained in knowledge, having made this plain to you in every respect, in all things (vv. 5-6).**

It is interesting to note that the word "untrained" which Paul used is an old word *(idiōtēs)* from which we get our word *idiot,* which Webster defines as an utterly senseless or foolish person. Paul was a great scholar and this enabled him to make a play on words to get a point across. His learning also enabled him to speak with philosophers without the use of equivocal or ambiguous expressions. He knew how to drive to the point of an issue in such a manner that all who heard him might understand. These "super-apostles," called by some "transcendent apostles," must have referred to the twelve apostles in Jerusalem. Did they (or any of them) visit the fields of Paul's labor? If there, were they engaged in missionary work away from home? We are not told about their labors in pagan lands, with the exception of Peter's. The brothers of Jesus did go out from Jersusalem and they apparently were a part of the Judaizing element. But as to whether they visited Corinth or not, we do not know. Maybe these "super-apostles" were a group of emissaries who went out from Jerusalem to check on Paul's work and who wound up as critics of his labors. At any rate, Paul made his point. Even if he were not an eloquent man in his use of rhetoric, when compared with the Greeks, he had knowledge beyond challenge.

Or did I commit a sin in humbling myself that you might be exalted, since I preached God's gospel to you free? (v. 7).

Some note a bit of sarcasm in Paul's words in this verse. For the Corinthians knew that Paul had accepted no honorarium from them incident to his preaching there. Still he was justified in raising the question about his self-support which he had dealt with at length in 1 Corinthians 9:1-18. Evidently his critics had not let the issue die down.

I robbed other churches, accepting material support for service to you (v. 8).

Paul used a strong hyperbole to get his point across; the old word translated "robbed," a word that literally means to despoil, or to strip arms from a slain foe. All that Paul did was to accept ration money such as would have been paid to a soldier for his service. But he disclaimed receiving any compensation whatever from the Corinthians for his ministry to them.

And when I was present with you, and in need, I was not a burden to anyone; for the brothers who came from Macedonia supplied my needs; and in everything I kept, and I will keep, myself from being a burden to you (v. 9).

Paul's word "robbed" could have been occasioned by his critics who implied that his living expenses had been made possible by gifts from the Corinthians, which was not true. He was in the loving care of the Macedonians, who expressed their concern in their gifts to supply his needs. This should have silenced the critics. But aside from that was Paul's firm resolve not to be a "burden" to the Corinthians, a point he had endeavored to make clear.

Because Christ's truth is in me, this boasting shall not be stopped in me in the entire regions of Achaia. Why? Because I do not love you? God knows. But what I now do, that I will keep on doing, that I may cut off the opportunity of those desiring an occasion to the end that in their boasting they may be found to be just as weak as we are (vv. 10-12).

The critics must have known even though they would not admit it, that the apostle was a man of integrity with a fierce spirit of independence, one who did not grasp after money. Were the feelings of the Corinthians hurt by Paul's rugged defense of independence which, however, did allow him to take gifts from the Macedonians and not from them? There is no way to answer this. On the other hand, his adversaries might have claimed, unjustly, that his refusal to accept support from the Corinthians might have been due to the fact that he felt inwardly that he was less than the "super-apostles" notwithstanding his claims. But it was time to bring to a close this angle of Paul's defense; so he began to speak fearlessly, in inflammatory terms about his accusers.

> **For such men are false, deceitful workmen transforming their appearance into apostles of Christ. And no wonder, for Satan himself changes himself into an angel of light. It is no great thing therefore if his servants disguise themselves as servants of righteousness, whose end will be according to their works (vv. 13-15).**

These words coming from the apostle were full of condemnation. Did Paul have more information about his accusers than he revealed? Had he been informed of the character of their personal lives? Were there moral inconsistencies in their own lives? Paul could hardly have uttered more insulting words concerning his critics. He pointedly charged that they were false apostles who disguised themselves so as to appear that they were "servants of righteousness." In branding them as servants of Satan, who was a specialist in the art of camouflaging, Paul reached deeply into the arsenal of invective such as the early apologetics employed. But Paul was tired of the spurious claims of these erring disciples, and decided to put an end to the discussion of the matter.

4. The Matter of Boasting (vv. 16-23)

> **Again I say, no one is to consider me to be foolish; but if not, receive me as foolish that I also may boast a little. What I am saying now, I speak not according to the Lord, but as in foolishness in this confidence of boasting (vv. 16-17).**

Paul resumed here what he called "foolish discourse" found in 11:1-6. He ignored his critics completely and went on with his boasting, reminding the Corinthians that his words were not to be interpreted as "according to the Lord." What he had to say was in full confidence that the Corinthians would finally grasp the sincerity of his purpose, though he had been impelled to employ an approach that on its face would appear to be foolish. He knew that some might interpret his words as being the result of pure *madness,* but he was still determined to go on with his boasting.

> Since many boast according to the human point of view, I will also boast. For gladly you who are wise put up with the foolish ones. For you put up with it if anyone enslaves you, if anyone strips you of your possessions, if anyone takes you captive, if anyone puts on airs, if anyone strikes you in the face. I speak to my shame, as though we have been weak; but in whatever way anyone would be bold (I speak foolishly) I am bold also (vv. 18-21).

These verses cover, in further measure, the character of those who opposed the gospel and the gospel messengers. Paul painted an arresting portrait of their mentality and behavior. In truth, they have often been downright boorish in manner, superficial, and full of self-interest. The picture is not a pleasing one. The same people who criticized him for his weakness tolerated the brand of accusers that Paul described in verse 20. His words actually amounted to condemnation of the Corinthians for putting up with these self-appointed critics, and without resistance, as they attempted to pull down the ministry of the apostle in their midst. Paul was unsparing in his words of reproof.

> Are they Hebrews? So am I. Are they Israelites? So am I. Are they the seed of Abraham? So am I. Are they servants of Christ? (I am talking as one beside himself), I am more than they; I have been in difficulties far more, in prisons even more, in beatings beyond measure, at death's door many times (vv. 22-23).

Here is a very telling part of the apostle's so-called "foolish discourse," in fact, the second one (11:21b-33). There were a few things about the apostle however, that his enemies could hardly criticize: he was a Hebrew, an Israelite, a descendent of Abraham. In verse 23 the apostle justified his sense of any superiority to which he might lay claim by comparing his own experiences with those of his enemies. Let them look at the matter any way they would, he had experienced more difficulties than they, had been in prison more often, had suffered "beatings beyond measure," and had been at death's door "many times." Who of them could say as much? Consider his words that followed:

5. Paul's Sufferings as a Minister of Christ (vv. 24-33)

> Five times I received from the Jews forty lashes, less one; three times I was beaten with rods, once I was stoned, three times I suffered shipwreck, I spent a day and a night adrift at sea (vv. 24-25).

These words, though they may be regarded as boasting, are not the product of a fictive mind; they simply recorded Paul's experiences at the hands of his enemies and in his journeys by sea. He went on to say:

> In my journeys I was often in dangers from rivers, in dangers from robbers, in dangers from my family, in dangers from the Gentiles, in dangers in the city, in dangers in the wilderness, in dangers on the sea, in dangers among false brothers, in labor and in hardship, in sleepless nights frequently, in famine and in thirst, in fastings often, in cold and in nakedness. And apart from the things I omit, I had the daily pressures on me of anxiety about all the churches (vv. 26-28).

In these verses the apostle gave more than a birds-eye view of the kinds of problems that he encountered on his missionary journeys. What interesting reading and inspiring examples we would have if Paul had been able to keep a daily diary of these events and to preserve them, as his letters were preserved, for future readers. The word "journeys" (v. 26) doubtless means travels on roads in contrast to travels on the sea. The much touted *pax Romana,* the plan for peace that Rome imposed upon her dominions, was perhaps no more successful, in many instances, than the effort of citizens in our day to live in peace behind their locked doors at night. Asia Minor was far enough removed from Rome to leave much to be desired in the matter of safety for travelers. They literally met danger wherever they went. The rivers were lacking in bridges in the waters where fords were not negotiable. The robber bands were likely those that attacked small groups of travelers or individuals in the country areas. Paul's dangers did not all come from these sources. His own people, as well as the Gentiles, gave him trouble. There were the false brethren—Christians who were critical of Paul and were actually his enemies. The Judaizers, of course, were ever active in their opposition to the apostle.

In verse 27 the character of the problems differs and the dangers are less acute. But the situation is, nevertheless, wretched. As with hardship and labor, there were nights in which he had no sleep because of circumstances. In his travels he was not always able to get potable drinking water or the necessary food to sustain him. In many of the areas through which he traveled, since there was no opportunity to get food, fasting was necessary. There is nothing to indicate in the text that the fasting was of a religious nature. His "in cold and in nakedness" reference was doubtless occasioned by his poverty. There were areas in which there were no shops where Paul could provide for his needs. But this was not all of Paul's burden. For he had the "daily pressures" of his "anxiety about all the churches." It was not just the church at Corinth that caused him to have anxiety; pressures came from all the churches that were under his care, for he did not take the pastoral side of his duties lightly. His worries were perpetual and his burdens were felt daily.

> Who is weak, and I am not weak also? Who is caused to stumble, and I am not inflamed? (v. 29).

The word "weak" that Paul used in reference to *weakness* may have referred to both spiritual and physical infirmity. (See Rom. 4:19; 14:1f; 1 Cor. 8:11-12; see also Rom. 8:3; 2 Cor. 11:21; 12:10; Phil. 2:26f.) Either the spiritual or the physical weakness will fit Paul's case. The word "inflamed" simply means that, when a brother stumbled, Paul is "set on fire" with grief (Robertson, *in loco*). His love for the brothers was almost overwhelming at times. He could not bear to see them fall victim to the snares of the trickery of the devil.

If I must boast, I will boast about the things that relate to my weakness (v. 30).

Paul made the open confession here that he had his own weaknesses, for he was human. The question of morality is not at issue. He had the "thorn" in his side, and one can only surmise as to the character of the thorn and the burden of it in his daily living. Paul's boasting, as a rule, was the kind of boasting spoken of in the Old Testament—boasting about divine help. But here boasting appears to relate to his physical weaknesses.

The God and Father of our Lord Jesus, who is blessed forever, He knows that I am not lying (v. 31).

Here again the apostle called God to witness to what he has been saying. "God knows," he said, "that I am not lying." Paul then went on to relate the Damascus experience and told of his ingenious escape.

In Damascus, the ethnarch under Aretos, the king, guarded the city of the Damascenes to arrest me, and through a window I was let down in a basket through the city wall, and I escaped their hands (vv. 32-33).

This event is recorded in Acts 9:24, though the details differ. In the Acts account, the Jews were the source of the danger, whereas here it was Aretos, the Arabian king. Of course it is entirely possible that the Jews and King Aretos worked together in the effort to arrest the apostle. King Aretos IV, then head of the Nabataean kingdom, east of Palestine, reigned from 9 BC to about AD 79. Damascus was one of those ancient cities, east of Palestine, that as well experienced in the fortunes of war. It had been in the hands of the Womans (63 BC), some think the city was captured by King Aretos in AD 34. This could indicate that Paul's Damascus experience could fall between AD 34 and 39. At any rate, Paul succeeded in his clandestine departure from the city.

[1]I must boast, though it is not helpful; rather I will come to visions and revelations of the Lord.

[2]I know a man in Christ, fourteen years ago (whether he was in the body or outside the body, I do not know—God knows), I know such a man that was caught up to the third heaven,

[3]and I know such a man (whether in the body or apart from the body, I do not know—God knows)

[4]that was carried into paradise and he heard unutterable words which are not permitted for man to speak.

[5]Concerning such a person as that, I will boast, but I will not boast concerning myself except in my weaknesses;

[6]for should I wish to boast, I will not be foolish, for I will tell the truth; but I refrain from doing so lest someone should count me to be more than what he sees me to be or what he hears from me.

[7]And by reason of the extraordinary character of the revelations, that I might not be exalted, there was given me a thorn in the flesh, a messenger of Satan, to torment me so that I might not exalt myself.

[8]About this messenger of Satan, three times I implored the Lord that he might go away from me;

[9]and He said to me, "My grace is sufficient for you; for my power is made complete in weakness." Therefore, I will boast all the more gladly in my weaknesses that the power of Christ may dwell in me.

[10]For this reason I delight in weaknesses, in mistreatments, in persecutions, in difficulties, in sufferings in behalf of Christ; for when I am weak, then I am strong.

[11]I have become foolish, but you have forced me to it; for I ought to be commended by you. For I have been in no way inferior to the super-apostles, even if I am a nobody.

[12]The distinctive signs of the Apostle have surely been done among you with every kind of patience in signs and wonders and powers.

[13]For in what respect have you been made inferior to the rest of the churches, unless it be that I myself did not burden you *with my living expenses?* Forgive me this injustice.

[14]Look, I am ready to come to you, and I will not be a burden to you; for I do not seek your material things, but you; for the children are not obligated to save up for the parents, but the parents for the children.

[15]And I will gladly spend and be spent in behalf of your souls. If I love you more abundantly, am I loved the less?

[16]So be it: I did not burden you; but by being a clever person, I took you cunningly.

[17]Did I take advantage of you through any of those whom I sent to you?

[18]I called upon Titus, and sent along with him the brother. Did Titus take advantage of you? Did we not walk in the same Spirit? In the same steps?

[19]You have been thinking all this time that we have been speaking to you in defense of ourselves. We speak before God in Christ; and all these things, beloved, are in behalf of your edification.

20For I fear that when I come I should find you not to be such men as I desire, and that I should be found by you not to be the sort of man you would wish, lest by any means there be strife, jealousy, anger, selfishness, slanderings, gossiping, big heads, disturbances;

21Lest in my coming my God should humiliate me again in your presence, and I should mourn over the many of those who had previously sinned and did not repent of their immorality and prostitution and sensuality which they had practiced.

12

Paul's Visions and Revelations

2 Corinthians 12:1-21

The theme of boasting extends throughout chapters 10, 11, and 12. Paul did not seem to get very far away from the idea, although he claimed that it was forced upon him by the Corinthians. Their blatant words of criticism and their heartless indictments had to be answered. Consequently he turned in his discourse to visions and revelations of the Lord.

1. Visions and Revelations (vv. 1-6)

I must boast, though it is not helpful; rather I will come to visions and revelations of the Lord (v. 1).

Paul had a feeling that the words he was about to utter would be of no special advantage to him, for nothing that he might say was likely to influence the Judaizers to any great extent. They were too stubborn in their thinking about him to alter their positions easily. But he would at least be on solid ground dealing with the visions and revelations that he had experienced. The word "revelations" (from *apokaluptō*, Rev. 1:1) means to *disclose, bring to light, reveal something that is hidden,* and in this instance it refers to divine revelation of the Scripture.

I know a man in Christ, fourteen years ago (whether he was in the body or outside the body, I do not know—God knows), I know such a man that was caught up to the third heaven, and I know such a man (whether in the body or apart from the body, I do not know—God knows) that was carried into paradise and he heard unutterable words which are not permitted for man to speak, concerning such a person as that, I will boast, but I will not boast concerning myself except in my weaknesses (vv. 2-5).

Paul plunged into a spirit of deep mysticism, a type of experience with which the Jews were not altogether unacquainted.
They were familiar with excursions into the supernatural realm,
and of course they knew about the final, bodily ascent of both
Elijah and Enoch. Paul did not deal with the dualistic philosophy
which distinguishes between the mystical concept of self in the
body of man from which self might be removed. Paul declared
that it was the man himself that was "caught up to the third
heaven" and that it was the same man that was "carried into paradise" where he heard unutterable words which it was not lawful
for man to speak. Paul professed ignorance about one side of the
experience, as to whether it was in or outside the body when all
this took place. The point is, he remembered the experience viv-
idly, as in contrast with the average dream which a person has in
the night; a dream soon passes away and is remembered no
more unless the person who dreamed continues to rehearse it in
his mind in order to give it a fixed place in the hall of memory.

Neither did Paul afford us any explanation concerning his use
of "the third heaven." The frequent use of the plurality of the
heavens *(ouranoi)* is merely in accord with the ancient usage of
the words "the heavens." Doubtless Paul might have given a discourse on the concepts of the apocalyptic riders and the rabbis'
use of the term. Revelation 2:7 indicates that the saved will be in
the enjoyment of paradise until the last day. But Paul did not
have to wait until the end of time to experience the glory of paradise for he was "carried [off] into paradise" where he heard the
"unutterable words." The expression "unutterable words *(arrēta
hrēmata)*" merely meant the words he heard were not to be spoken for the simple reason that they were inexpressible. Such
words were beyond human powers to utter for they were words
too sacred to tell. The word "unutterable" *(arrēta)* does not mean
that human tongue was not able to utter such words, for that was
not the point. They were words that it was not lawful, or permitted, for man to speak.

Paul left us greatly in debt to heaven for further knowledge
about the experience. For that matter, many of the great supernatural experiences of the children of God are recounted without

explanation. The only thing we know about the time of the experience was that it was "fourteen years ago." Certainly it was a mountaintop experience in the life of the apostle, an experience so sacred that he dared not share it in any further detail. It would have been truly wonderful had Paul recounted in some detail his experience in paradise. But then he would have gone beyond the bounds of the words of Jesus in His own reference to paradise. Jesus did not go into detail in His discussion of paradise, and neither did the apostle.

> For should I wish to boast, I will not be foolish, for I will tell the truth; but I refrain from doing so lest someone should count me to be more than what he sees me to be or what he hears from me (v. 6).

Paul's words in these verses in no way reflect thinking on his part concerning any dual personality. Again that is not the point of his words. He merely dealt with two aspects of his being in which God was able to impart to him special revelation. Paul was still a man (*anthrōpos*) when he received that divine revelation, a supreme manifestation of God's grace bestowed upon him in that supernatural experience. Paul declared there would be no boasting about that experience, but rather if he were disposed to boast, his boasting would have to do only with himself and his "weaknesses." Paul no doubt was thoroughly familiar with the terminology of the mysticism of the pagan religions, but his words here do not relate to such, except perhaps to cause some of his reasons to recall pagan concepts of the mystics.

Paul's modesty and quiet reserve are openly manifested here. His reticence in dealing with the matter of his revelations is due to the fact that he wanted to be judged purely on the basis of what he was—what people saw about him and heard from him—and not what someone had said about him. Paul did not want anyone to overestimate him as an apostle. He wanted only the facts to be used by those who would pass judgment on his ministry.

2. A Thorn in the Flesh (vv. 7-10)

> And by reason of the extraordinary character of the revela-

tions, that I might not be exalted, there was given me a thorn in the flesh, a messenger of Satan, to torment me so that I might not exalt myself (v. 7).

Paul's use of the plural word "revelations" could refer that the "thorn" came as a result of the special revelation of which he had just spoken, or that it was a safeguard against self-exaltation because of all of the visions and revelations which he had had. The point was, the "thorn" (an old word meaning *stake, splinter, thorn*) was given to him for the distinct purpose that he might not exalt himself. What the character of the thorn was, no one knows. There have been all kind of surmisings. Some thought it was migraine headaches, epilepsy, insomnia, and others. But all we know is that it was an affliction that troubled Paul in the flesh; and that the thorn came to him so that he might not exalt himself. It is difficult for any man not to think of himself more highly than he ought to think when the circumstances that surround him are surpassingly favorable or when he comes to have the feeling that he surpasses others in his knowledge of things and his ability to deal with the issues of life.

About this messenger of Satan, three times

> **I implored the Lord that he might go away from me; and He said to me, "My grace is sufficient for you; for my power is made complete in weakness." Therefore, I will boast all the more gladly in my weaknesses that the power of Christ may dwell in me (vv. 8-9).**

The fact that the apostle implored the Lord to cause the thorn to leave him forever indicates the serious character of his suffering from the thorn. He evidently had the feeling that the presence of the thorn would hinder his effective ministry. He wanted nothing to interfere with the mission to which he was called in Damascus. The word "torment" is from an old Greek word *kolaphizō* which literally means *to strike with a fist, cuff, beat someone,* or *roughly treat someone.* So whatever the action of the thorn was, it was a source of perpetual *torment* for Paul. But the answer of the Lord was enough for Paul: If God's grace was "sufficient" for him, and if God's "power" was made complete in weakness, then he could go on and boast even "more gladly" in his weakness to the end that he might experience the indwelling power of God in his life.

> For this reason I delight in weaknesses, in mistreatments, in persecutions, in difficulties, in sufferings in behalf of Christ; for when I am weak, then I am strong (v. 10).

Paul's words here, no doubt, appear paradoxical to many. How can a man delight in such torments as Paul experienced in the presence of the thorn? Grandiose feelings? Hardly. In the assurance that came to him from the Lord and in the course of his own reflections on the sufferings of Jesus, the apostle was delighted that he could follow in His sufferings. The word "mistreatments" signifies *haughty injuries, insolent actions*. What is more, Paul declared that these interminable sufferings that issued in weaknesses in the flesh afforded him the opportunity to gladly boast in his weakness, knowing that in such circumstances he would experience the indwelling power of Christ more fully.

3. Paul's Continuing Concern for the Corinthian Church (vv. 11-21)

> I have become foolish, but you have forced me to it; for I ought to be commended by you. For I have been in no way inferior to the super-apostles, even if I am a nobody (v. 11).

In fact, Paul insisted that in the light of everything the Corinthians knew about him and had witnessed about him, there should have been no need for him to boast or to glorify himself. There had evidently been words of criticism that attempted to downgrade his character as an apostle in comparison with the twelve. Paul flatly declared that he was "in no way inferior to the super-apostles." At any rate, Paul's critics had been uncomplimentary of him. There would have been no reason for his words of boasting had the vicious attacks of those who wanted to decry his ministry not put him in a position of self-defense.

> The distinctive signs of the Apostle have surely been done among you with every kind of patience in signs and wonders

and powers. For in what respect have you been made inferior
to the rest of the churches, unless it be that I myself did not
burden you *with my living expenses?* Forgive me this injustice (vv. 12-13).

One need not endeavor to find sharp distinctions between
Paul's words "signs and wonders and powers." All of them related
to the supernatural aspects of God's dealings with Paul and with
the Corinthians themselves. They had witnessed these distinctive
claims of the apostleship and had seen that all of them had been
marked by constancy as though there had been no letter. The
apostle's words here amount to a gentle rebuke, as if to say,
"Marks of the true Apostle have been witnessed, again and again
in your midst, and you have seen signs and powers and wonders; yet you continue as carping critics." Obviously Paul felt that
there had been jealousy on the part of the Corinthian church in
relation to the other churches that Paul had served. The only
basis Paul could see for their jealousy was that he did not burden
the Corinthians with his living expenses. Was there a bit of sar-
castic irony in those words at this point? At least he asked them
to forgive him for "this injustice."

> Look, I am ready to come to you, and I will not be a burden to
> you; for I do not seek your material things, but you; for the
> children are not obligated to save up for the parents, but the
> parents for the children. And I will gladly spend and be spent
> in behalf of your souls. If I love you more abundantly, am I
> loved the less? (vv. 14-15).

Who among the false apostles could make claims such as Paul
made here? What little he had in the way of material possessions,
or in the resources of his own physical and spiritual self, he was
ready to spend all for the souls of the Corinthians. By his words
in self-defense, the apostle laid down a maxim that has carried
down through the centuries with great meaning for parents: "For
the children are not obligated to save up for the parents, but the
parents for the children" (v. 14). Paul's words were indeed tender
and loving, and they reflected his compassionate regard for the
Corinthians and all of those to whom he ministered. The words

"save up" *(thēsaurizein)* mean to *save, store up, gather up.* The analogy that Paul used as to father-child relations means that Paul looked upon his converts as his "spiritual children." He felt a deep and abiding responsibility concerning their spiritual welfare and, so far as he was concerned, whatever he had in the way of money, energy, time, and love, he was ready to expend in behalf of the welfare of the souls of his people.

> So be it: I did not burden you; but by being a clever person, I took you cunningly. Did I take advantage of you through any of those whom I sent to you? I called upon Titus, and sent along with him the brother. Did Titus take advantage of you? Did we not walk in the same Spirit? In the same steps? (vv. 16-18).

Paul's enemies evidently had accused him of taking this offering for himself or perhaps using Titus as his intermediary. So then the implication was that through the offering the apostle was exploiting the Corinthians. Paul could have not been more forthright in dealing with the matter. But while he had asked the Corinthians for nothing in behalf of himself, he had, "being a clever person," asked them for their support in the offering for the poor saints of Jerusalem. There is no reference here to the identity of the brother he sent along with Titus. Paul acknowledged the fact that he had called upon Titus and the brother to go to the Corinthians on his behalf, and then he put on the Corinthians the burden of answering the question: "Did Titus take advantage of you? Did we not walk in the same Spirit? In the same steps?" The attitude of Titus was in no sense different than the attitude of Paul. Paul was eager to defend Titus against such false insinuations as had been made of him. He made his defense without apology. Paul and Titus were one and the same in motive and in their conduct. They had walked together "in the same Spirit [and] In the same steps."

> You have been thinking all this time that we have been speaking to you in defense of ourselves. We speak before God in Christ; and all these things, beloved, are in behalf of your edification (v. 19).

We have in this verse what Robertson called a "progressive present indicative." Their feeling this way about him had been going on for a long time. The time had come for Paul to put a stop to it. Therefore he called to witness "God in Christ" and told the Corinthians that, instead of taking advantage of them in behalf of himself, everything he had done was "in behalf of [their own] edification." His mission had been to build up, not to tear down, to be of benefit to others with no advantage to himself personally in the interrelationships. From the standpoint of self, Paul claimed these words to be "selfless."

> **For I fear that when I come I should find you not to be such men as I desire, and that I should be found by you not to be the sort of man you would wish; lest by any means there be strife, jealousy, anger, selfishness, slanderings, gossiping, big heads, disturbances (v. 20).**

The word translated "gossiping" means *whispering, talebearing,* when used in the bad sense. It is a onomatopoeic word used of the "sibilant murmur of a snake charmer" (Robertson, *in loco;* Eccl. 10:11). Paul painted a graphic picture of what had been going on in Corinth in his absence, doubtless with a major part of it slanted critically toward his ministry there. Any one of the vices was enough to disrupt the fellowship of the church and to call in question anyone against whom the invectives were directed. The picture is a rather disturbing one and causes one to wonder if there are such vices in any considerable measure in the Christian churches of our day.

> **Lest in my coming my God should humiliate me again in your presence, and I should mourn over the many of those who had previously sinned and did not repent of their immorality and prostitution and sensuality which they had practiced (v. 21).**

The vices listed by Paul recall Galatians 5:20 and also the terrible picture of the vices painted by Paul in Romans 1:29ff. Such vices are deadly in their impact on the unity of a body of believers. This verse apparently recalls the preceding visit of Paul (10:1). He did not want to be humiliated again because he did not want to mourn over his congregation again and to be ashamed of them before God in their presence. He had no way of knowing, of course, how many of them had previously sinned and had not repented of their immorality, prostitution, and sensuality. But Paul knew that sins in this realm have a progressive nature and that many offenders, if they have practiced these sins for a long time, may not be delivered. Of course, Paul had made it clear that the door to repentance and reconciliation was always open to the offender while there is life. The Christian who has engaged in the efforts of reconciliation, can truly say, "While there is life, there is hope."

[1]This is the third time I am coming to you; at the mouth of two witnesses or three every word shall be established.

[2]I have said before, and I say now, as I did when present the second time, and now being absent, for those who have heretofore sinned, and to all the rest, that if I come to you again I will not spare,

[3]since you are seeking a proof of Christ speaking in me, who to you is not weak, but is powerful in you.

[4]Although he was crucified out of weakness, He lives by the power of God. For we also are weak in Him but we shall live with Him by the power of God toward you.

[5]Test your own selves whether you are in the faith; keep on testing your own selves. Or do you not understand that Jesus Christ is in you? (unless indeed you do not stand the test!)

[6]But I hope that you will come to know that we are not failing to stand the test.

[7]And we continue to pray to God that you will not do anything evil, not that we may appear approved, but that you may do the good, though we fail to stand the test;

[8]for we are not able to do anything against the truth, but for the truth.

[9]For we rejoice when we are weak, and you are strong; this we also continue to pray: that you be made complete.

[10]Because of this, being absent, I write these things that, being present I may not act sharply according to the authority which the Lord gave me for building up and not for *tearing down*.

[11]From now on, brothers, be joyful; continue to mend your ways; be conciliatory; hold the same opinions; live in peace; and the God of love and peace will be with you.

[12]Greet one another with a holy kiss. All the saints greet you.

[13]The grace of our Lord Jesus Christ, and the love of God, and the fellowship of the Holy Spirit be with you all.

13

Final Words of Warning and Greeting

2 Corinthians 13:1-14

The apostle began the last part of his discourse in this letter in a formal, judicial manner. Starting with a quotation from Deuteronomy 19:15, he issued a warning that there is to be formal inquiry, conforming to legal procedures, in which there will be no evasions. It is interesting to note that he emphasized the fact that all testimony will be supported by two or three witnesses. This is to be the third visit of the apostle, and from the latter part of verse 2 "that if I come to you again," Paul surrounded the visit with a contingency, for his words "if I come to you again" amount to a third-class condition. On the first visit the church was founded (1 Cor. 14:15; 9:1). The visit was described in Acts 18:1-18. The second visit was the one he recalled *with sorrow* for then he was confronted by the adversaries who apparently began to attack him. He then dealt, as chapter 13 reveals, with the third proposed visit.

1. Paul's Third Visit to Corinth (vv. 1-3)

This is the third time I am coming to you; at the mouth of two witnesses or three every word shall be established (v. 1).

The full text of Paul's reference to the law in Deuteronomy reads as follows: "One witness shall not rise up against a man for any iniquity, or for any sin, in any sin that he sinneth: at the mouth of two witnesses, or at the mouth of three witnesses, shall a matter be established" (Deut. 19:15). This means that any matter dealt with at this formal inquiry would be unassailable—not open to assault or attack, not subject to dispute or denial. The apostle had had enough of that. He wanted the issue of this inquiry to be final. Jesus recalled the same principle of decisions

151

dealing with problems between brothers in the faith in Matthew
18:16. Whenever there is ecclesiastical discipline, it should be
carried out in a proper manner, a manner that will leave no
grounds for dispute.

> **I have said before, and I say now, as I did when present the
> second time, and now being absent, for those who have here-
> tofore sinned, and to all the rest, that if I come to you again I
> will not spare (v. 2).**

These words are due to the fact that his apostolic authority had
been questioned by his rivals. He wanted no more of that, for he
had gone to great lengths already to qualify and to declare his
role as divinely called, and divinely instructed on all procedures.
The words "said before" referred to the second visit, while the
words "I say now" have reference to the letter which he is writing
in absentia and which not only recall the stern words in
2 Corinthians 12:21, but also reinforce his determination not to
spare unrepentant brothers and all the rest who had helped to
bring about the disturbing conditions in the Corinthian church.
This time there would be no leniency. The matter would be dealt
with openly, at face value.

> **Since you are seeking a proof of Christ speaking in me, who
> to you is not weak, but is powerful in you (v. 3).**

Did Paul's words here suggest that the Corinthians themselves
had become testy, irritably impatient, touchy? It certainly appears
so. For, obviously, some of his critics had called upon him to offer
proof, in a further way, that he was an authentic messenger of
Christ who was delivering Christ's message. What is more, the
Corinthians evidently felt that in a debate concerning Paul's apostolic authority, they would come out as winners. Because of this
disposition on the part of his critics, he would remind them all the
more of the strength of Christ and of the power of Christ manifest
in their midst.

2. Christ's Crucifixion (v. 4)

> **Although He was crucified out of weakness, He lives by the**

power of God. For we also are weak in Him but we shall live with Him by the power of God toward you.

In Christ's crucifixion, His humanity was in the foreground, and in the weakness of that humanity He was crucified. All the while, of course, He had all authority and power. He did not have to yield to the adversaries in the awful moments incident to His arrest in the Garden of Gethsemane. He could have called in authoritative power to bring His enemies there to a complete standstill, even to annihilation. But He did not. While He was crucified "out of weakness," He continues to live by the power of God. The apostle, sharing in that weakness, also declared his confidence in the full benefits of life with Him "by the power of God toward you."

In this verse the apostle set forth the fundamental doctrine of the Christian faith, namely, the atoning death of Christ on the cross and His resurrection from the dead. The death and resurrection of Christ are accepted by believers as historical events that are unquestionable—the footing or foundation on which all Christian faith is established. In this confidence the feet of believers may be place securely, with eternal stability. It is the basis of entrance into the new life, the new relationship with God in Christ, in the new position with reference to society. Christ's victory over Satan with all his power brought about at the time of the victory a "cosmic upheaval" that issued in the eternal keystone in the arch of Christian faith. The apostle himself experienced a measure of that "cosmic upheaval" on the Damascus Road. And this is true of every believer who, moved by the Spirit of God, has claimed access to the new life of fellowship of God in Christ.

3. A Challenge to Self-Examination (vv. 5-10)

Test your own selves whether you are in the faith; keep on testing your own selves. Or do you not understand that Jesus Christ is in you? (unless indeed you do not stand the test!) (v. 5).

Here Paul challenged his opposition in Corinth to turn the critical searchlight on themselves. He reminded them that they might reverse the process in which they had been so adamantly engaged in their effort to bring him down if they looked at their own consciences and examined themselves with the same type of criticism with which they had attacked him.

Paul said that they were to do their own testing, implying that he was willing to let the case rest with their findings. He did not suggest that what they declared as the result of the testing be established in the mouth of two or three witnesses. He also said that the testing was not to stop. And he went on to say, "Do you not understand that Jesus Christ is in you?" Of course, if the Corinthians failed to pass the test themselves, they would be disqualified to participate in a theological dispute that involved the basic concept of faith, namely, the death and resurrection of Christ.

> **But I hope that you will come to know that we are not failing to stand the test (v. 6).**

These words of Paul should have been awakening words, for they were words that the Corinthians needed desperately to hear. The verb Paul used here *(gnōsesthe)*, meaning *come to know,* implied that there was yet optimism in Paul's regard for the Corinthians. It was obvious that they had not yet come to know that Paul and his companions were not failing to stand the test. But it was necessary for them to come to know this fact, else his witness in their midst would have little meaning. Paul's added word reveals with clarity his broad knowledge as a teacher without being pedantic. He was not overly concerned with the minutiae of formalistic reasoning. His appraisal of their ability, and his hopes for their future understanding, made it clear that the door to such was open and that he had hopes that one day they too would stand the test.

> **And we continue to pray to God that you will not do anything evil, not that we may appear approved, but that you may do the good, though we fail to stand the test; for we are not able to do anything against the truth, but for the truth (vv. 7-8).**

As the apostle turned to words of assurance that his prayers would continue in behalf of the Corinthians, he revealed the hope of his prayer and the motive for it; "that you will not do anything evil." Why did he engage in such prayer? Does it give the Corinthians the impression he and his co-workers might "appear approved"? Not at all. The motive of the prayer was that the Corinthians themselves might "do the good," even though Paul and his co-workers could "fail to stand the test." Paul wanted the Corinthians to act in such a way that they would merit the approval of God in doing "the good," irrespective of the consequences of their own regard for him as to whether or not he and his co-workers passed the test in their sight. Paul's words have the ring of sincerity. At stake was approval of him and his co-workers in the eyes of the Corinthians. The real issue lay in the character of their response to good and evil. After all, is not this the crux of the matter for all followers of Christ? And at the final day, will not the individual Christian be judged by his response to the challenge of good and not evil? Paul went on to say that he himself could do "[nothing] against the truth." Please recall his words in Romans 1:18 where he said that "evildoers may hold down" the truth of God through their evil deeds, but that the holding down can only hinder or retard the implementation of the truth of God in human hearts. In the end, truth will prevail. Notice how Paul's words throughout the Epistle are punctuated with Christian maxims, guidelines for fruitful, Christian living. And Paul illustrated these maxims in a marked degree. Here there appears no tinge of selfishness in his approach or in any earthly rewards, whether at the hands of either his friends or his enemies. His concern for the salvation of all persons was his priority. Paul made it clear in his words about truth that he could never doubt, or engage in battle with, the truth of God or any matter that had been fixed by God as a guideline for His followers.

> **For we rejoice when we are weak, and you are strong; this we also continue to pray: that you be made complete (v. 9).**

Paul then summarized his thoughts about what had gone before (13:1-8). As far as any weakness on his part was concerned, he rejoiced in it. He knew that he had access to all the power, all the strength he would ever need in God; and he declared his personal sense of rejoicing in the strength of the Corinthians. He wanted it to be known that there was no jealousy in his heart. But the real thrust of verse 9 was in the motive of his rejoicing and his prayer in behalf of the Corinthians. He wanted to see them "made complete." He wanted to see them become mature Christians, believers who no longer needed to be fed merely the milk of the gospel. He desired to see them strong enough to receive solid food. Paul's words "made complete" come from an old word *(katartisis)* which carries a sense of completion, being made complete. That is what Paul wanted to see realized in the Corinthians. All of this, Paul was confident, would come to pass if the Corinthians would face the issues realistically, take hold of themselves, and follow their Christian conscience in their action in the world about them rather than to be under the ruling guidelines of the world.

> **Because of this, being absent, I write these things that, being present I may not act sharply according to the authority which the Lord gave me for building up and not for *tearing down* (v. 10).**

Paul clarified his own position in facing the trying problems brought upon him by the Corinthian church. While yet away he wrote to assure them that, when he did come for the visit, his desire was not to "act sharply," not withstanding his authority to do so; and he gave as the reason for his intended course of action his desire to act in accord with the authority the Lord gave him "for building up and not for tearing down." Paul had no desire to assume the role of an iconoclast even when dealing point blank with those who were in error theologically or whose unbeliefs had been in some way affected by the superstitious beliefs of the pagan world in which they lived. Paul attempted to deal with these erring brothers and sisters in the meek and gentle character of Christ. There were times, of course, when the apostle had to be bear down hard on his erring "children" but he did it in love, for their welfare. His continuing obsession was to build up and not to tear down and so to hold forth the word of truth that unbelievers, everywhere, might become believers in Jesus Christ as Savior and Lord. Paul's words "[deal] sharply" are from an old adverb *(apotomōs)* which means rigorously, severely, as in correcting someone or something.

4. Final Exhortations, Greetings, and Benediction (vv. 11-14)

From now on, brothers, be joyful; continue to mend your ways; be conciliatory; hold the same opinions; live in peace; and the God of love and peace will be with you (v. 11).

Paul's closing greetings and exhortations called on the Corinthians to practice a noble, upright life-style. He challenged them to be joyful, to keep on rejoicing, to continue to be creative in that they would keep on mending their ways in choosing good against evil. He called upon them to be conciliatory in their relations with one another to the end that each one might find in the other encouragement and comfort—two aspects of the Christian life-style. He encouraged them to deal with problems, as they doubtless would arise in the future, and face them realistically and impartially, until they could come to share the same opinions. He called upon them to live in peace with the abiding assurance that "the God of love and peace" would be with them.

Greet one another with a holy kiss. All the saints greet you (v. 12).

It was the custom for the sexes to be separated in public gatherings. The men sat in one place and the women in another. In greetings, the men kissed the men, and the women, the women. It seems that this became also the custom among Christian. Jean Herring translated the word usually translated as "a holy kiss" (hagiōi *philēmati*) "the Christian kiss." I do not find a Greek word with the meaning assigned to it by Herring, and I believe the better translation is "a holy kiss." The word "holy" *(hagiō)* in the cultic sense, means dedicated to God, sacred, holy; and this came to have the meaning of *pure, perfect, worthy of God* (Bauer). In things, *holy* carried the sense of dedicated to God, sacred. The words "All the saints" referred to the Christians round about the location from which Paul sent the Epistle to the Corinthians. The Jews in Paul's day regarded the kiss as a gesture of reconciliation. This ritual, however, seems to have doubtful desirability with some of the early Christians, and later Christians as well. Robertson called attention to an act of the Archbishop Werter of York of England in 1250 which produced among his people a "pax-board," in which the clergy kissed first, and then passed around to the people *(in loco)*. One wonders how popular such a "kissing tablet" would be in our day!

The grace of our Lord Jesus Christ, and the love of God, and the fellowship of the Holy Spirit be with you all (v. 13).

This is a beautiful, and fitting benediction to this stirring epistle. In it Paul recognized the presence of all the Trinity. Did Paul write this final word of greeting in his own hand? He did so in 2 Thessalonians 3:17, as he told us, but he does not tell us here whether it was written by his emanuensis or by himself.

You will notice how Paul began this final word of greeting with the words "The grace of our Lord Jesus Christ." Without the grace of the Lord, there can be no genuine love of God, and no fellowship of the Holy Spirit. The grace of God precedes everything that issues in the Christian life-style, beginning with salvation. Did not Paul say, in his Epistle to the Ephesians, "For by the grace ye have been saved through faith; not out of you; it is the gift of God; not of works, so that no one may boast" (Eph. 2:8-9)? And this grace of Jesus Christ comes as a free gift to all who will look to Him by faith and in a sincere desire to come to know Him and to follow in His steps. The word translated "fellowship" *(koinōnia)* was the idea of *communion, fellowship, association,* and *close relationship.* It is used of the marital relationship which is the most intimate experience that there is between husbands and wives. In this relationships the human and the divine joined together on the pinnacle of Christian religious experience.

Bibliography

A brief bibliography of books that may be found helpful in the further study of 2 Corinthians:

American Standard Version. New York: Thomas Nelson and Sons, 1901.

Archbishop, Trench. *Synonyms of the New Testament*. Kegan Hall, Trench, Trubner, and Co. Ltd.

Barrett, C. K. *The Commentary on the Second Epistle to the Corinthians*. New York: Harper and Row Publishers.

Bauer, Walter. *A Greek English Lexicon of the New Testament*. Second Edition, Chicago and London: University of Chicago Press.

Bernard, J. H. *The Second Epistle to the Corinthians, Expositors' Greek Testament*. Grand Rapids: Wm. B. Eerdman's Publishing Co.

The Broadman Bible Commentary. Volume 11. Nashville: Broadman Press, 1971.

Brooks and Winbery. *Syntax of New Testament Greek*. Washington, D.C.: University Press of America, 1979.

Davis, W. Hersey. *A Grammar of the Greek New Testament*.

Fausset, A. R. *Bible Cyclopedia*. Hartford, CN: The S.S. Scranton Co., 1960.

Herring, Jean. London: The Epworth Press, 1967.

Hunter, Archibald M. *Introducing the New Testament*. Philadelphia: The Westminster Press, 1957.

The Interpreter's Bible. 12 Volumes. Nashville: Abingdon Press, 1952.

Kittel, Gerhard. *Theological Dictionary of the New Testament*. Grand. Rapids: Wm. B. Eerdman's Publishing Co. 1967.

Liddel & Scott. *A Greek English Lexicon*.

Nestle's Greek New Testament. London: British and Foreign Bible Society, 1937.

Robertson, A. T. *A Grammar of the Greek New Testament in the Life of Historical Research*. Nashville: Broadman Press, 1934.

Robertson, A. T. *Word Pictures in the New Testament*.

Souter. *A Pocket Lexicon to the Greek New Testament*.

Thayer. *Greek-English Lexicon of the New Testament*.

Vincent. *Word Studies in the New Testament*.

Wescott and Hort. *Greek New Testament*.